THE WALRUS SAID

By the same author:

Heritage of Help, Robert Hale 1992

Captains of the Gates, Robert Hale 2001

THE WALRUS SAID:

A Long Silence is Broken

Denis Blomfield-Smith

The Book Guild Ltd
Sussex, England

First published in Great Britain in 2004 by
The Book Guild Ltd
25 High Street
Lewes, East Sussex
BN7 2LU

Typesetting in Baskerville by
Keyboard Services, Luton, Bedfordshire

Printed in Great Britain by
CPI Bath

A catalogue record for this book is available from
The British Library

ISBN 1 85776 812 4

The Walrus and the Carpenter
　　Were walking close at hand;
They wept like anything to see
　· Such quantities of sand:
'If this were only cleaned away,'
　　They said, 'it would be grand!'

* * *

'The time has come,' the Walrus said,
　　'To talk of many things:
Of shoes – and ships – and sealing-wax,
　　Of cabbages – and kings – '

Through the Looking Glass and
What Alice Found There
Lewis Carroll (Macmillan, 1872)

Contents

List of Illustrations and Acknowledgements of Sources

(between pages 72 and 73)

1　St Edmund's Abbey before the Reformation (The Bury Past and Present Society)

2　Bronze doors at Benevento Cathedral (The Conway Library, Courtauld Institute of Art)

3　Framlingham Castle (National Monuments Record, English Heritage)

4　St James' Tower at Bury St Edmunds (National Monuments Record, English Heritage)

5　The 'Bury Bible' – part of the frontispiece for Jeremiah (The Master and Fellows of Corpus Christi College, Cambridge)

6　The 'Bury Cross' The Easter Plaque (The Metropolitan Museum of Art, The Cloisters Collection 1963. Photograph by Malcolm Varon© 1988 The Metropolitan Museum of Art)

7　The 'Bury Bible' – The opening page (The Master and Fellows of Corpus Christi College, Cambridge)

List of Maps and Diagrams

Foreword

By Dr Christopher de Hamel

This is a tale about medieval works of art of the highest importance. The first, which is in my care in the Parker Library at Corpus Christi College, Cambridge, is a vast illuminated manuscript Bible, now bound in three volumes, which was written and decorated at the Benedictine monastery of Bury St Edmunds around 1130. It contains extraordinary pictures and decorated initials, filled with people, animals, birds and monsters. It is brilliantly coloured and the pages sparkle with pure lapis pigment and burnished gold. The Bury Bible, as it is called, is one of the most spectacular surviving English Romanesque books, and it is important not only because of its beauty and imaginative invention, but also because it is unusually well-documented. The chronicles and other medieval records of Bury describe how the book was painted by the 'incomparable Master Hugo', who also made other works of art for the Abbey, including bronze doors for the west front of the Abbey church and a cross for the monks' choir. Hugo is the earliest English professional artist whose name is known. He was clearly a man of diverse talents and his work was greatly admired.

The bronze doors survived until the sixteenth century, when they were probably melted down. The Bible, too, evidently remained at the Abbey until the suppression of the monastery under Henry VIII in 1539, and, like other books from Bury St Edmunds, it was sold or given away at the Reformation. It was acquired, probably indirectly, by Matthew Parker (1504–1575), Queen Elizabeth's first Archbishop of Canterbury, who entrusted it to Corpus Christi College in 1574, where it has remained ever since. The cross, however, is never mentioned again. It is the principal subject of the investigations of Brigadier Blomfield-Smith.

Two aspects of this tale are absolute fact. The first is that a cross made by Master Hugo did exist at Bury St Edmunds in the twelfth century, and it is no longer there. Something has to have happened to it. That is certain. The other is that a magnificent medieval carved cross turned up in eastern Europe in the mid-twentieth century, and it is now in the Cloisters Collection at the Metropolitan Museum of Art in New York. It is certainly twelfth-century and its quality is not in doubt. It has to have come from somewhere. That too is certain. We thus have the beginning of a story and the ending of a story. Whether the two connect is the subject of the present book.

There are certainly stylistic similarities between the Bible and the cross. Both include stocky figures of saints and prophets and soldiers, with big staring eyes and sinuous bodies cloaked in swirling drapery. Both include graphic narrative scenes and Latin inscriptions on scrolls. Illustrated manuscripts are rare enough from the first half of the twelfth century but carved ivories of this date and quality are almost unknown. It is therefore exceedingly difficult to make judgements as to whether the same hand could have made both. The techniques of painting and carving are very different. Both the cross and the Bible are strikingly Byzantine in style, even though we know that the Bible, at least, was demonstrably made in England. It seems likely that Master Hugo may actually have seen Greek art, probably icons and perhaps even the mosaics and frescoes of Sicily, Cyprus or Byzantium itself. This was the early period of the crusades. Hugo was not a monk (he is called 'Master', not 'Brother' in the monastery records). It is possible that he had been a part of one of the English expeditions to the Holy Land, and that he returned to England with experiences or even drawings of Byzantine painting and carving. The tale recounted in *The Walrus Said* takes up the history of the crusades in the following generation and it suggests that Hugo's cross itself might actually have been carried back the other way, eastwards in the crusading armies of Richard Coeur-de-Lion. It is a marvellous and eye-opening account of a very great period of European history, romance and chivalry. It makes the survival of the Bury Bible, still kept 30 miles from where it was made, seem very unadventurous indeed.

Christopher de Hamel
Donnelley Fellow Librarian
Corpus Christi College

Acknowledgements

Any literary structure which endeavours to bridge a gap of eight hundred years of silence must have vulnerable areas where a degree of shoring up is necessary, and the bibliography included in this book represents a store of support which has been indispensable in telling this story. I am grateful for the knowledge, skill and research of those who have provided these sources.

I have quoted extensively from The Reverend Charles Dodgson's little masterpiece of nonsense and philosophy 'The Walrus and the Carpenter' because it seems to me to be so astonishingly apt to events so totally remote from what Alice found through the looking glass: or perhaps, on a deeper level, not so far removed after all!

It was the Dean of St Edmundsbury Cathedral, The Very Reverend James Atwell, and Dr Sally Dormer, university lecturer and mediaeval art historian, who inspired me, in their different ways, to attempt this venture, though they are in no way responsible for its shortcomings which are exclusively mine.

I am especially indebted to Dr Christopher de Hamel for

being prepared to spare time from a very busy academic life to write such a lively and meaningful introductory foreword for my book. To have the real interest that Dr de Hamel has shown, from one so uniquely associated with Master Hugo's work, has been very heartening and is greatly appreciated.

I owe special debts of gratitude to Dr Charles Little, the Curator of Mediaeval Art and The Cloisters at the Metropolitan Museum of Art in New York and to Dr Christopher de Hamel, the Librarian of the Parker Library at Corpus Christi College, Cambridge for all their help in so many ways; to András Barabas, Professor Ronald W. Zweig and Colonel and Mrs Howard Stephens for all their practical efforts and advice in matters Hungarian; to Philip Ward-Jackson of the Conway Library in the Courtauld Institute of Art for his research; to the Suffolk Institute of Archaeology and History for so willingly providing technical advice; to clerical and medical friends for advice in their specializations; to Peter Dow for his early encouragement of this project; to Philip Judge for his excellent maps; to the staff of the Suffolk Library and Record Office at Bury St Edmunds for taking such pains; to all those who have so helpfully provided illustrations and who are recognised individually elsewhere; and last but not least to Dr Thomas Hoving for providing not only a vivid and gripping account of his pursuit of the walrus ivory cross, but also for unwittingly furnishing part of the foundations of this work.

As always, there would have been no book without my wife's support in countless ways.

Preface

Among the grave goods discovered in 7th-century burial mounds at Sutton Hoo in Suffolk were the remnants of a magnificent silver helmet, probably belonging to one of the Kings of East Anglia. There were sufficient fragments of the helmet for archaeologists to be able to reconstruct the helmet as it had been. I have attempted in this book to carry out a similar operation with the story of the unique walrus ivory cross currently in the Cloisters Museum at the New York Metropolitan Museum of Art.

The long silence about this cross lasted some eight hundred years and it can be no surprise that the sounds emerging from it have been faint and intermittent. The disappearance of the cross from the 12th to the 20th century and the extreme secrecy maintained by the dealer who acquired and sold the cross have meant that parts of this story must inevitably be conjecture. Nevertheless, the record I have made of this period constitutes, I maintain, a history. I have taken as my precedent the definitions of annals, chronicles and history set out by no less an authority than the Regius Professor of Modern History in the University of Oxford and Librarian to the Archbishop of Canterbury and editor of the *Chronicle of the Reigns of Henry II and Richard I*, William Stubbs. In his preface to that work he propounds his view that history:

> 'whether according to its earliest use it may have been an exposition of the results of research, or of the process of the research itself, it was now understood to mean an exhibition of events in their deeper relation of cause and effect, in their moral and political bearing, and in an approach to a dramatic or pictorial form.'

Stubbs recognised that, in chronicles, 'There is none of the life or of the colouring of history; there is no "word-painting" or grouping of characters, or pictorial effects; there is none of the philosophy of history, no speculations on principles.' Fortified by such an authority I have called this personal interpretation of these scraps of evidence a history.

The Abbey of Bury St Edmunds, as the shrine of St Edmund, the martyred King of East Anglia, was the chief place of pilgrimage in England until the murder of Thomas Becket resulted in Canterbury superseding it as the primary shrine, at least politically. Nevertheless, St Edmund's Abbey remained one of the largest, and most influential monasteries in England; and the fourth richest. It was favoured by successive monarchs and, on the other side, was probably the venue for a preliminary meeting by barons to draft the Magna Carta before confronting King John with it at Runnymede.

The riches and power of the Abbey in contrast to the hard life and poor situation of the townspeople led to riots in the 14th century, and to successive attacks on it culminating in the sacking of the Abbey in 1381 during the nation-wide 'Peasants' Revolt'. The Abbey recovered from this and re-established its control until the dissolution of the monasteries by Henry VIII in 1538/9. The Abbey was destroyed, and the stone from the great buildings was looted for use in buildings and walls by the townspeople so that only the underlying flint can now be seen in the few ruins visible. These ruins have never been systematically investigated archaeologically, and time, and the freedom of all to make what use of them they wish, is leading to further deterioration. So little respect, let alone reverence, is apparent from both townspeople and those responsible, that it is almost as if there is regret that earlier destruction was not more thorough. Thus all that can be treasured and wondered at of the great Abbey (which the Borough trumpets in its publicity) is the 'Bury' Bible and the ivory cross, both wonderful 12th century works of art from the hands of England's first known professional artist, Master Hugo.

The bare bones of the verifiable knowledge about the 'Bury' cross are as follows: in 1955 there appeared on the world's art market a small masterpiece in the shape of a cross of walrus ivory. Every part of the cross was carved with biblical figures and scenes, and such was the brilliance of the sculpting that its maker had clearly been a truly exceptional master of his craft: not only that, but there were strong indications that his was a talent

imbued with scholarly knowledge rather than that of a highly
skilled artisan under instruction from a cleric.

The cross was indisputably of English origin and, on the
evidence of the detail of the carving, dating from the 12th
century. However, the walrus tusk itself, from its carbon dating,
had already been at least five hundred years old when its sculptor
began his work. The fact that the cross had survived when such
a vast amount of religious art had disappeared as a result of the
Reformation, Henry VIII's decrees and the acts of Cromwell's
men was an indication that it had almost certainly left England
before the 16th century.

Indeed the cross re-appeared from Middle Europe. It was
offered for sale in 1955 by a Yugoslav with an Austrian passport.
This man was a collector and dealer, whose opportunities had
included being part of a Yugoslav mission at the end of the
Second World War with the task of recovering works of art looted
or otherwise dispersed in that war.

The collector refused to disclose how the cross had come
into his possession, with one result that the British Government
would not provide funds for the British Museum to acquire what
would have been a national treasure. The cross was eventually
purchased by the Metropolitan Museum of Art in New York and
is in the Cloisters Treasury there.

As a result of research into the origins of the cross a story
has emerged of the Yugoslav acquiring the cross in pieces from
a monastery in Eastern Europe. That there is some substance in
this is indicated by the independent evidence of a Hungarian

who asserts that in the early 1930s he had seen the cross in the possession of a local priest in a Cistercian monastery in Zirc in Hungary. Without prior knowledge of the Yugoslav's story, he also described the cross as being in three or four pieces, and by a title which indicated a knowledge of some of the special inscriptions on the cross unlikely to be known by anyone who had not seen it. His description included the reference to papers held by the priest which pointed to the cross having been taken on a crusade by a soldier.

A further clue in the search for evidence of the whereabouts of the cross during Hungary's turbulent history from the 12th to the 20th centuries may have been revealed by Dr Thomas Hoving, who acquired it for the Metropolitan Museum of Art in 1963. He recorded that when he took the cross 'completely apart': 'I was rather shocked to find in one of the splits a hideous black encrustation of a kind I had seen before only on objects I found in graves on a dig in Sicily in 1956. I wonder if the cross could have been found in a grave.' This gives extra substance to the story of the cross when seen in the 1930s because it was described then as being of 'blackish ivory'.

On the finding of such fragments the final shape depends.

In the end, though, for those who have looked on this cross of walrus ivory, and so have felt its magic, it speaks for itself and tells its own story.

SELECTIVE GENEALOGY OF EUROPEAN RULERS

11TH AND 12TH CENTURIES

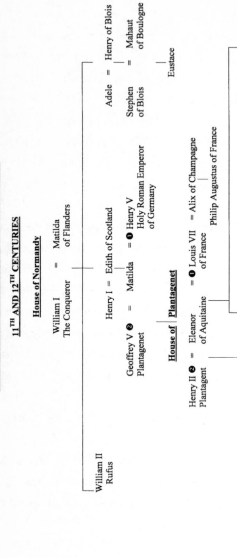

CHAPTER 1

The Beginning

As he looked out from his house by the river at the great bulk of St Edmund's Abbey appearing grey in the morning mist, Abbot Anselm must have had moments of nostalgia for the white stone of St Saba's in Rome gleaming in the morning sun. On occasions like that though, the great additions that he had been able to bring about in the somewhat stark and minimal structures he had inherited from his predecessor must have assisted his own self-discipline in dispelling any regrets.

In his more than twenty years as Abbot since his election in 1121, there stood to his credit, and to the great skills and dedication of his sacrists Hervei and Ralph and to the brilliant artist and craftsman, Hugo, whom he had brought from Rome, the completion of the great nave of the Abbey, stretching from the west front almost to the river, the church dedicated to St James and the great carved bronze doors in the west front (so reminiscent of St Saba's). St Edmund's Abbey was now more than able to justify, to the townspeople who depended so much upon it and to visiting pilgrims, its role as the shrine of England's patron saint and the primary place of pilgrimage in England.

Hugo's accomplishments since his arrival at the Abbey had already more than justified Anselm's decision to bring him to England. In addition to the great west doors and a bell for St James, he had just completed a bible which Hervei had commissioned for Talbot, the Prior, in which the draughtsmanship and illustration were beyond compare.

Anselm's period as Abbot had not been easy. From the ecclesiastical point of view he had benefited to some extent from being the nephew of Anselm of Canterbury, the late Archbishop, and consequently had had good support from Rome. On the secular side, however, the running battles between Queen Matilda, Henry I's daughter, and Stephen, the Conqueror's grandson, made for disruption in the countryside and considerable difficulties for a national institution like the Abbey.

The Benedictine Abbey had been founded by King Cnut a hundred years before, and had been richly endowed with land and privileges. In administering its wealth of land and buildings and the inhabitants of these, it still depended greatly on authority delegated by the Crown. Consequently, close relations with the reigning monarch were very important for the proper maintenance of law and order and the prosperity of the large area under the Abbot's suzerainty. At times, under King Stephen, conditions approaching anarchy were sometimes present in the countryside round Bury St Edmunds, and it was inevitable that some of this instability was felt both in the town which had grown up round

ST EDMUND'S ABBEY LANDS IN SUFFOLK

the Abbey, and in some of the Abbey's own estates. On some
occasions the King would be calling for help to advance his cause,
either in money, kind or knightly service. On others it was needful
for a responsible Abbot to be prepared to deploy his knights
(Anselm could call on more than a score of these) or his support
from Rome, or both, to resist the depredations of some of
Stephen's lawless bands.

In these days it was not even possible to rely upon support
from ecclesiastical sources. Bishops took sides. The Bishop of Ely,
siding with Matilda, was at odds with the Bishop of Winchester,
who supported Stephen, with the result that much of the Ely
monastery land was ravaged by the protagonists of one side or
the other. At St Edmundsbury these events tended greatly to
distract the cellarer and sacrist from their duties, both as
administrators and Abbey officers, since they both had clear
responsibilities for governing, respectively, the manor lands and
the borough. For his part, Abbot Anselm was not only referee in
such matters but also the local judiciary. For some Abbots and
their immediate staff, these secular commitments were meat and
drink, but Anselm's strength lay on the spiritual and aesthetic
aspects of his vocation and the same was true of Hervei, his
sacrist. As a result, these two chief figures at the Abbey were on
duty for very long hours indeed, adhering strictly to the traditional
Benedictine horarium extending to sixteen hours in the winter
and nearly eighteen in the summer, but having somehow to meet
most of their secular commitments outside these programmes.

Although neither Anselm nor his sacrist would voice their

regrets publicly, the three to four hours allowed in the programme as working time, as against daily liturgy and devotions, were never sufficient to fulfil the ambitions which they had for the development of the aesthetic side of the Abbey as well as the welfare of the monks, the administrative staff and the local tenants and townspeople. The Abbot, as a favourite of Rome, was called upon to spend much time on papal duties out of England. It was in this respect that Anselm must have blessed his decision to bring Hugo with him. Here was a man not only possessing unique skills in working with his hands in almost any medium, but also seeming to have an innate sense of spiritual rightness; gifts which enabled Hugo to produce artefacts of wonderful quality and spiritual appeal without the detailed direction and supervision that any ordinary craftsmen would need. After the presentation to him of a concept, he needed only the gentle feeding of ideas, occasional prompting and encouragement to bring brilliant work to fulfilment.

The satisfactory position as regards the structural and decorative aspects of the Abbey, however, was not mirrored by the environment which it dominated. The Abbey owned most of what is now known as West Suffolk[1] and the material and spiritual welfare of very large numbers of tenants, townspeople and Abbey servants depended on the Abbot and his officials. Quite apart from the Abbot's clear moral responsibility for all their souls, the existence of a contented population would be reflected within the Abbey

---

[1] Together with large estates in neighbouring shires.

precincts and ensure prosperity within and without. Two aspects of life in England at that time made it a pressing task for the Abbey to find a way of leading those who depended on it into a more well-grounded and contented way of life. The first of these was that at this time people looked to the monks, not only as the guardians of their saint, but also as their only intercessors. The second was that the instability of the countryside under King Stephen made the need for material help and good administration vital.

Throughout his abbacy Anselm must have been very conscious that, for many of the local Anglo-Saxons, his foreign origins tended to give the impression of an emotional temperament, an interest in the more ostentatious aspects of Christian life and an impatience with the more mundane day-to-day problems. It is fair to assume, however, that a man of his intelligence and experience would have done his best to compensate for this and approach policy matters in particular in a measured fashion.

The circumstances in which the Abbey found itself in the 1140s were that while those most concerned with the material well-being of the Abbey's dependants, notably the sacrists and the cellarer, were working very hard and, on the whole, dealing adequately with all the secular problems, the Abbey was failing to provide for a very large number of the, largely illiterate, population the essential strength of faith and understanding needed to support them in times when loyalty, trustworthiness, and fair dealing were so often threatened, and anarchy and barbarism sometimes prevailed.

The Abbey was open to all and very many from outside its walls were able to have contact with monks and officials. These, by their example, undoubtedly provided strength for some, and such artefacts as Hugo's splendid Bible would certainly give inspiration to those with sufficient education. This, however, was a minority and there was clearly a great need for an evangelistic instrument which all could understand.

One of the modern conditions which was militating against the maintenance of good and close relations between the Abbey and its dependants was the replacement of the earlier barter arrangements by monetary systems of rent and purchase. The use of coin had, to some extent, corrupted both sides and led to the incurrence of debt and to consequent borrowing from Jewish money-lenders, with all the disruption of honest, friendly relationships which resulted. In so far as the monks and servants of the Abbey were concerned, the encouragement by usurers to acquire hitherto undreamed of inessentials was both undermining the straightforward simplicity of their living and cultivating a false relationship between the religious and secular life of St Edmundsbury.

The increasingly currency-based trading was also causing the time spent by the Abbey staff on administration to rival, or even to surpass, that devoted to worship and the religious enlightenment of the tenants and townspeople.

Reversing the trend towards this reliance on money rather than barter was never a possibility but a better balance was likely to be achieved with a greater emphasis on bringing the public more into the devotions and prayer; making the most of the real reverence for saints' relics to underline the value of the monks as intercessors. So the Abbey policy became to allow the populace even more freedom within the Abbey and to encourage tenants, their workforce and the townspeople to understand more about the Abbey's life and purpose.

There remained the question, however, of how much of the Christian story the very limited education of most visitors would enable them to absorb. A significant decision emerged to meet this problem.

The concept of the whole Christian story told pictorially and so realistically as to require little interpretation is one which might arise in many a cleric's mind. Some might see a series of pictures, others perhaps a tapestry format, but to envisage a cross depicting the Christian story in three dimensions from Adam and Eve to the crucifixion and resurrection demands a combination of intellect, imagination, artistic flair and skill of the highest order. This synthesis happened to exist at Bury St Edmunds in the 1140s in the persons of an Abbot, who was the nephew of a saint, a sacrist of great spiritual awareness and an artist of unique talents, Master Hugo; and a truly marvellous artefact was conceived.

The creative instincts of Master Hugo further extended the evangelistic potentiality of this masterpiece. Among the treasures which remained in the sacristy from the founding of the Abbey by King Cnut were some walrus tusks; undoubtedly regarded by some as interesting Scandinavian relics, but with little useful purpose. For the remarkable trio at St Edmund's Abbey they must have now appeared as a gift from God. For Hugo they presented a wonderful material for carving his masterpiece, and for Anselm and Hervei a perfect way to renew after a hundred years the association between King Edmund, the patron saint, and King Cnut, the Abbey's founder. A more powerful evangelical instrument for the 12th century would be difficult to envisage.

The practical difficulties which confronted Hugo were enormous. Morse ivory was brittle and the amount available limited, so there could be very few mistakes. Also the size of the cross would be governed to some extent by the comparative shortness of the tusks, so that even a relatively small cross would have to be constructed in four or five parts. It is possible that Hugo had seen a well-known Ferdinand and Sancha carved ivory cross in Spain which may have helped to kindle his ideas, and will have shown how the most might be made of an ivory surface. Even so the task which Hugo had set himself must have been a daunting one, even for a great craftsman.

CHAPTER 2

'Getting it Clear'

A state bordering on anarchy existed in East Anglia from 1140 onwards as a result of the fight for the English crown between Matilda and Stephen. Ambitious and greedy barons chose whichever side they considered likely to bring them more treasure and land; and changed to the opposing side if that appeared to be likely to triumph. An earl or baron who found himself frustrated in his ambitions was wont to vent his rage on the nearest helpless citizens and countryside. The most unpleasant and unprincipled in East Anglia was, almost certainly Geoffrey de Mandeville. Initially a supporter of Stephen for the price of the earldom of Essex, he transferred his loyalty to Matilda, only to return to Stephen's fold when Matilda's mistakes and arrogance once more rendered her's to be a lost cause in the east, although still having ample support in the west country. In the end Geoffrey de Mandeville played the field once too often and was charged with treason by Stephen. True to type, he used his castles in Essex as a ransom for his release and subsequently took out his anger on the inhabitants of the Cambridgeshire fens. With his bands of mercenaries and bandits of all types he ravaged, burnt and ransacked the whole area, destroying virtually all sources of decent living for all, including Cambridge itself and the Abbey at Ramsey. Fortunately he was killed by an arrow whilst so engaged and died in September 1144. He was, however, not alone in using the struggle between King Stephen and the Empress Matilda as an excuse for utter lawlessness.

The main protagonist in the Bury St Edmunds district was Stephen's son, Eustace, who, following de Mandeville's pattern, laid waste much of the area including some of the Abbey's estates: this in spite of the general support for King Stephen by the East Anglians. The difficulty of any degree of certainty about stability in any particular area of England in this period of anarchy was that individual owners of estates and land inflicted their current personal enmities on their local areas, without regard to the support or otherwise which the inhabitants might be giving to the major figures. For the people at this time, who were finding it hard enough to make a living in a country wasted by endless fighting and despoliation, England was a perilous place, with starvation as much a threat as violent death from marauding bands.

When no one could be sure as to who was a friend, a monastic establishment which could rely on powerful patronage provided a precious sanctuary. Some were too directly involved on one side or the other because of local landlords but St Edmundsbury Abbey was secure and its officers were determined to keep it so, and to provide the tenants and citizens around with a place of refuge when needed.

Throughout most of the 1140s there were sometimes whole families within the Abbey gates and, except at certain times, there was almost complete freedom for the local people to wander through most of the monastery buildings. It was this freedom which Hugo's cross could exploit by being exposed to as many non-Christians as possible, that they might receive the message of real Christianity to counter the numerous offences committed in its name in England and elsewhere.

With that situation in mind the message which the cross would need to bear had to be clear and uncompromisingly strong; and so it was.

The vertical part of the cross represents the core of life; traditionally the tree of life and the natural source of the True Cross. The tree of knowledge had, after all, been the start made by Adam and Eve who had ascended it for its fruit; ultimately a tree had yielded Christ's resurrection. The 'old Adam's' ascension had brought sin and death: the ascension of the 'New Adam' had brought redemption and resurrection. Inevitably, therefore, at the base of the tree Hugo carved Adam and Eve in their primitive form and, at the top, Christ's ascension.

Even making full use of the thickness of the tusks, working on the front and back and using both sides for inscriptions, the space available for the task of telling the whole Christian story was limited and there must have been very difficult decisions to make as to what to omit. It was clear that the role for the cross, if it was to fulfil its task, must be for it to be displayed where all sides could be seen and if possible to be used as a processional cross on occasions.

Subjects which clearly had to be included were the events of Good Friday and Easter and, as in the Spanish example, Hugo made use of plaques at the ends of the crosspiece for these and the plaque at the top of the cross for the Ascension.

The linking of the Old and New Testaments is strikingly demonstrated on a roundel in the centre of the cross and it is a scene which both Anselm and Hugo would have remembered from their time with Abbot Suger at St Saba's: Moses and the serpent in the desert. The raising of a brazen serpent by Moses was a sign of redemption from the threat of the poisonous snakes which the Jews regarded as punishment for their sins.

The roundel is a pictorial representation of Christ's words to Nicodemus, 'As Moses lifted up the serpent in the desert, so must the Son of Man be lifted up' and includes that quotation from John as well as others from both testaments. The unbroken chain is maintained with figures of the Old Testament prophets and New Testament evangelists on the back of the cross, with an appropriate quotation accompanying each.

In these early days of this creation of the Hugo cross came the shock of the re-conquest by the Turks of Edessa and the expulsion of all the Frankish forces from the whole of that district of Syria. As a result of this set-back to the successes of the First Crusade there was a noticeable spread of hostility in the West to all heathens. There must have been some (and one's thoughts incline towards Samson, the sub-sacrist for one) who would have wanted the scenes portrayed to point a much more dramatic and accusing finger at the Jews as the murderers of Christ. If so, it would seem likely that Anselm would have reminded them of the purposes of the cross as both a symbol of Christianity and an instrument for conversion rather than a weapon of revenge: also that it was God's will in the great cycle of events that His Son should be sacrificed in order to achieve man's redemption.

There was no concealing of the Jewish role in the story. The dispute between Pontius Pilate and Caiaphas, the High Priest, about the reason for the crucifixion as recorded above the cross, and the traditional representation of the Synagogue as the opponent of the Church, were both present on the cross as they were in the event.

When the difficulties of working the relatively small walrus tusks and somehow fitting them together to make an intricately carved whole were taken into account, the task facing Master Hugo was indeed formidable.

There was a prodigious amount of work going on in the Abbey throughout the second half of Anselm's abbacy at Bury St Edmunds, the greatest part of this being the completion of the great nave and the church of St James which was built in place of the old basilica of St Denis. This meant that Sacrist Hervei and his successor Ralph were very preoccupied and that Hugo was left much to his own devices in further work on the cross, though he too was frequently committed to elements in these major works. His mentor in moments of difficulty was Anselm, with whom he dealt directly and whose spiritual and liturgical knowledge and sensitivity were consequently stamped on the work.

Because of the diversions both within and outside the Abbey, it was not until 1147 that the cross was nearing completion. Hugo had needed a remarkable degree of concentration to carry out his truly complicated plan, to involve the monks in confirming biblical history and appropriate quotations, and to consult frequently with the Abbot and the Prior. It had been an exhausting commitment, but he knew he could not afford to delay its completion for too long because so much of the inspiration for it had been Anselm's, and the latter's health was failing.

Indeed towards the end of the 1140s Anselm became less and less able to fulfil all his duties and many were performed by Ording, who had earlier acted as Abbot when Anselm, having been proposed as Bishop of London, was of necessity away during the selection period. In the event, to everyone's great distress, Abbot Anselm died before the cross could be completed and dedicated, and he was succeeded by Ording in 1148.

It is likely that the new Abbot would have needed a considerable amount of enlightenment about the cross from its creator. Certainly Ording would have understood the main scenes and symbols representing the liturgy for Holy Week and the conventional representation of the evangelists, Mark, Luke and John as the lion, ox and eagle respectively on the left, right and top terminals of the cross (though he might have needed some prompting to find Matthew on the back of the cross reporting Christ's words about Jonah next to that prophet himself). Equally, the central roundels of Moses lifting the brazen serpent before the Israelites in the desert and Christ as the lamb with the Jewish lance point resting below the wound on its breast, are not likely to have needed any elaboration. In the realm of the inscriptions, however, some help may have been needed by the Abbot who was described by a great Bury monk and chronicler as '*homo illiteratus*' (no scholar).

The words in large lettering on the front and sides of the vertical shaft of the cross in particular may have posed some problems – as they have in subsequent times.[1] There was nothing wrong with Ording's knowledge of the Bible though, and once the relevances of these to the linking of the Old and New Testaments and the symbolism of the tree had been shown, his own consciousness of the difficulties of language would have made him appreciate the problems of being able to condense into couplet form words to complement the story on the cross. The central roundel with the figure of the lamb with its breast pierced by the Synagogue lance, with the quotation from St Paul's letter to the Galatians, 'cursed is every one that hangeth on a tree', would be clear to him as an example of symbolism of 'Christ hath redeemed us from the curse of the law' while also pointing up the essential significance of the 'tree'.

It seems likely that, after some further clarification of the numerous inscriptions on the cross, the Abbot would have

---

[1] See Chapter 12.

appreciated its message as well as the craftsmanship involved in it. It must be doubted, however, whether he would have continued to give it the same importance in the role of the Abbey as had his predecessor, particularly in the light of the developing situation.

The year 1148 was one of major changes in the world outside the Abbey. As well as seeing the last of a great Abbot, England saw the last of the widow of Henry I, the aggressive Matilda. Her son, Henry Plantagenet, made one rather half-hearted effort in 1147 to support her campaign in England to depose Stephen, but by 1148 they were both back in Normandy. Matilda had lost the majority of her important supporters among the earls and barons, and others who might have enjoyed continuing a life of warfare were tempted instead to profit from fighting the Moors in Portugal.

A factor which began to show itself likely to disturb the calm in the country with the end of the fighting over the throne was the stirring up of anti-Jewish, or perhaps more accurately anti-heathen, feeling. The murder of a boy in Norwich, which had caused something of an agitation there in 1144, was given very wide publicity, stretching to the continent of Europe, by one Thomas of Monmouth from 1150 onwards. Thomas, who subsequently became a monk in Norwich Cathedral Priory, expanded greatly on the original charge made by the boy William's uncle that the murder was a ritual one by Jews, carried out as a copy of Christ's crucifixion. In the climate of the times this story was willingly grasped on very scant evidence and resulted in the boy's acceptance, at first in Norwich and later in East Anglia, as a saint, though really this was only observed liturgically at Norwich.

Thomas's *Life of St William* which ran to seven volumes eventually (although William lived for only twelve years) undoubtedly did much at this time to incite sectarian violence against the Jews who, since the squabble over sovereignty in England, had lost much of the Royal protection they had enjoyed under King Henry I.

The capture of Edessa by the Turks and the miserable failure of the Second Crusade to redress matters were events that had already produced a climate in England in which hate for 'heathens' was easily revived. It was a situation by no means only of English origin. At the time of the First Crusade there was a great deal of violence against Jews by crusaders in France and the Rhineland. A Cistercian monk, engaged on recruiting for the crusade in many cities in these areas, was urging Christians to attack not only Muslims abroad but Jews in Europe, as being other enemies of Christ. All this sectarian violence hardly needed any particular incident to ignite it, so a child murder which could be attributed to Jews, however slight the evidence, was bound to provide ample fuel. It is only surprising that at Bury St Edmunds the impact was relatively slight.

All the same, there were other, more mundane, reasons for the Jews in Bury St Edmunds to be likely to become victims in Ording's time as Abbot. The ravaging of the countryside by the rival barons supporting Stephen or Matilda, the pillaging of towns and farms and the large rural areas, where the outcome was that no work was done, resulted in widespread hardships and famine. Many of the farms and estates which belonged to the Abbey could no longer provide revenue, either in money or in kind. The Jews, as the only element permitted to loan money, and at this time one of the few sources still having the means to do so, were becoming more and more the creditors to the cellarer, the sacrist and other officials and individuals in the Abbey. In these days, as thereafter, lenders were destined to be blamed and hated.

Abbot Ording's priorities were very different from those of his predecessor. He had inherited from Anselm an Abbey of splendid ecclesiastical buildings including two fine churches and towers, and great works of art from Hugo. Ording's interests were more in the day-to-day welfare and the facilities provided for the monks and novices. He did not possess Anselm's level of education or his evangelistic fervour and, as a result, the Abbey assumed a more prosaic and introspective aspect. The previous policy of encouraging the townspeople and tenants to spend time within the Abbey and its precincts fell into disuse. There were many Jews within the Abbey walls from time to time but they were there on financial business and little effort was made to convert them (other than, that is, towards more moderate terms). The original purpose behind Hugo's superb masterpiece in miniature, the walrus cross, was pursued no longer, and the cross was placed on the altar in the monk's choir.

Perhaps the commissions which Master Hugo appears to have had from Abbot Ording best symbolise the change in the character of the Abbey of St Edmund with the death of Anselm. A large, simple wooden cross for the rood screen and statues of the Virgin and St John for the monk's choir were the result, and may well have been the most appropriate items at the time.

Sacrists also tend to change with abbots, and Ording brought in his nephew, Helyas, in that role. The inspired Ralph and Hervei were men of the past, and the spiritual and artistic life of the Abbey became the poorer in consequence.

CHAPTER 3

'Of Shoes and Sealing Wax'

It was perhaps fortuitous that the Abbey had an essentially practical Abbot when it suffered a serious fire in the early part of his abbacy because this severely damaged the type of domestic buildings which were Ording's forte. The chapter house, infirmary, dormitory, refectory and abbot's hall all had to be rebuilt and provided the main tasks for Ording and Helyas in the 1150s.

A serious and prolonged effect of this fire though, was the cost of the rebuilding adding to the already poor state of the Abbey's finances. The continuing poverty in the rural areas had a natural and immediate impact on the town where the market and the associated traders could do little business. Everyone was borrowing; few were paying their debts. Obligations to the Jewish usurers were growing and feeling against them rising in direct proportion.

There was some relief, however, in a reduction of the actual mayhem in the countryside but it would be some time before the country estates and farms would have recovered sufficiently to resume proper payments of rents to the Abbey. Also, although King Stephen was not now having to devote all his time and resources to defending his throne, the task of administering the land over which he was sovereign (never his strong point) was proving beyond him. One of the results of this was that Jews were prospering because they were not being tapped for what amounted to their royal 'protection money', but by the same token they were much more at risk, bereft of royal protection.

It was not surprising that there was little in the way of great art or literature added to the possessions of the Abbey at Bury St Edmunds at this time, although somehow, perhaps with Jewish money, sufficient funds were raised for the production of a silver frontal for the high altar.

The Europe-wide reputation of St Edmund's Abbey for the next twenty-five years would consist of past glories. Its great days had been those of Baldwin and Anselm. Not only were they great Abbots with most talented supporters, but they both had the enthusiastic backing of ruling monarchs and pontiffs. There is little doubt that in their time the Abbey's writ had the weight of royal or Vatican edicts. However sound an organisation resulted from Abbot Ording's solid administrative skills, he was missing wholehearted support from both King and Pope. King Stephen and Pope Eugenius III were enemies: the latter being a strong supporter of the Anjou royal family as represented by Queen Matilda and her son Henry Plantagenet; the former opposing the Pope at every opportunity. Abbot Ording, having taught Stephen in his younger days and having subsequently maintained regular contact through correspondence, found the King's complete break with the Roman Church an obstacle now to any close relationship between himself and King Stephen. Stephen, for his part, always found it difficult to make decisions and consequently was inconsistent in his treatment of St Edmund's Abbey.

Ording's two distinguished predecessors, Baldwin and Anselm, had also possessed considerable prestige and power from their position as great feudal leaders. Their lands extended to eight and a half 'hundreds'. Their tenants were, in many cases, military and, certainly in one case, with royal connections. In times of prosperity and the undisputed dominance of the current sovereign, this feudal strength, when added to close relations with Rome, gave the Abbot the authority of a provincial ruler. Abbot Ording was never to enjoy the luxury of this situation. While he was Abbot he did a great deal to try to reduce the cultivation of much of the wasted land and to regulate the excessive borrowing upon which tenants and tradesmen were tempted to embark. To achieve success in this without influential backing from King and Church was a lengthy task and Ording had only eight years before he died.

Sadly for all the very many people of the countryside and town of Bury St Edmunds, Hugh, who succeeded Ording as Abbot, although a kind man and a good monk, was weak, easily led and a hopeless manager, particularly as regards external administration. Instead of continuing with Ording's tight regulation, conditions of laissez-faire were quickly in place. To raise money, land was sold off cheaply, estates broken up, woods and forests were felled indiscriminately for timber, and buildings were neglected. These being short-term answers, loans were still needed on a large scale and for very many this was the start of a vicious circle in which further borrowing was reached to pay the very high rates of interest demanded, since securities came to be in very short supply.

The Abbey itself suffered, both from lack of funds to maintain it and from the lack of discipline and devotion among the staff and some officials who generally gave the minimum effort. Individuals pawned robes and artefacts that belonged to the Abbey and, in general, corruption and fraud became widespread. Even those who had the interests of the Abbey at heart, like Abbot Hugh's sacrist, William, acted wrongly, although his motive was good. In order to enable the treasury building in the Abbey to be properly repaired, he entered into a bond with a Jew from Norwich which eventually amounted to £1,200, excluding interest. Official seals belonging to the Abbey were used to authorise these large borrowings, and either carelessness or corruption ensured that news of the poor state of affairs was kept from those outside with responsibilities towards the Abbey – and, if possible, from the Abbot himself; though the latter borrowed widely himself. At the time of Abbot Hugh's death there was not just one Abbey seal being used for pledging the Abbey's credit but thirty-three.

Abbot Hugh's end followed the unhappy pattern of his abbacy. On his way to pray at Thomas Becket's shrine at Canterbury he fell off his horse in Kent and dislocated his knee. His kneecap was displaced and doctors never succeeded in restoring it, his leg became infected and eventually, in spite of the care given him at the Abbey, his heart was damaged and he died in November 1180.

The ill-discipline that had been rife during Abbot Hugh's life continued, since all his personal belongings were stolen and only the items which could not be removed from the Abbot's house were left. Even the convention that there should be some small contribution to the poor for the good of the Abbot's soul could not be followed. William, the sacrist, claimed that he had already had to subsidise the Abbot's household and could do nothing.

It was, perhaps, a final commentary on the depth to which the once great Abbey had descended that there was no attempt to nominate a successor for Abbot Hugh for two years. This was a neglect which might have resulted in the Abbey deteriorating even further if it had not been for a very lively and conscientious sub-sacrist – Samson. With no Abbot, the Prior, Robert, was in charge of the Abbey; a monk with a very amiable disposition whose main ambition was to keep everyone happy. If all his subordinates had maintained high standards of honesty and behaviour this benevolent attitude might have done little harm, because during Abbot Hugh's reign, while generally rules were lax and ill-discipline rife, the Abbot would often select offenders in an arbitrary fashion and punish them in a draconian way. In his time few knew where they stood: under Prior Robert all knew that most conduct was acceptable. The sacrist, William, who might have mitigated their state of affairs, instead took the maximum advantage of the situation, spending funds on the inconsequential and completely neglecting his duties of maintaining and improving the Abbey's property. His assistant, the sub-sacrist, Samson, in contrast was very active. Quite apart from ensuring that the workmen under his control carried out all necessary repairs, he arranged for a choir-screen to be made, decorated with paintings and accompanying elegiac verses which owed much to Hugo's cross in the monk's choir.

Samson also set in motion the building of a tower for the west end of the Abbey church, including obtaining some of the building materials for it. Such activity by a relatively junior official, which contrasted so markedly with his superiors and others around him, was bound to result in mistrust and resentment. Samson and one of the monks helping him were accused of misappropriating funds to finance the tower and, by the efforts of the sacrist, a ban was put on the use of funds for any purpose other than the payment of the very many debts owed by the Abbey. Samson, for the time being, was thwarted.

The strangest aspect of the Abbey situation at this time was the failure of the King to appoint an abbot to replace Abbot Hugh. Henry II and Queen Eleanor had restored order to their kingdom, on both sides of the Channel, by 1156. Henry was on very good terms with the Church, both in Rome and in England. The Pope was a strong supporter of the Angevin royal household and the relationship between the Church in Rome and in England had never been closer. Yet, although the King had been notified immediately of Abbot Hugh's death, and may have been aware of the Abbey's failings, he made no move towards appointing a replacement.

The state of affairs within Henry's kingdom, however, was certainly a preoccupation for him at this time and for some time to come. His territory stretched from the Scottish border to the Pyrenees and within this there remained many powerful enemies of the House of Anjou. Because the loyalty of those on whom Henry needed to count was personal to him, it was important for him to present himself sufficiently often to the various parts of his realm: Normandy, England, Ireland, Aquitaine, Brittany, each had to be visited as often as he could. There were numerous local uprisings in Henry's continental possessions throughout the second half of the 1160s but in 1173 a more serious rebellion began. This was inspired by Louis of France, anxious for the return of some of his provinces and making use of the acquisitiveness of Henry's sons, Henry and Richard. They were dissatisfied with nominal possessions represented only in their titles, and encouraged by Queen Eleanor, their mother, who attracted men of all ages – and trouble – with equal facility and enthusiasm; and there were always barons and mercenaries happy to join in on the prospect of plunder and promises of reward. The main blows as far as England was concerned came from Scotland, whence the Scottish King, William, and his younger brother David invaded on the promise of land and title from young Henry Plantagenet. King William was captured and this attack came to nothing.

MEDIEVAL SUFFOLK
SHOWING LIBERTY AND HUNDRED BOUNDARIES

LIBERTY OF ST EDMUND -
ST EDMUND'S ABBEY LAND

LIBERTY OF ST ETHELDREDA-
ST ETHELDREDA'S ABBEY, ELY LAND

GELDABLE-
REMAINED UNDER ROYAL JURISDICTION

Liberty boundary

Robert Beaumont,[1] Earl of Leicester, was the leader of the other invading force, about two thousand strong and largely composed of Flemish mercenaries; if truth be told this was more in the form of weavers who were economic migrants rather than experienced soldiers. This force landed on the north bank of the River Orwell estuary with little or no opposition and rendezvoused with Hugh Bigod, Earl of Norfolk, another rebel, and his retainers at his castle at Framlingham. They made an unsuccessful foray to the city of Dunwich whence they retired, chastened, to Framlingham. They did succeed in razing a small castle at Haughley but by then Humphrey de Bohun, England's Constable and Richard de Lucy, the Justiciar had returned from the Scottish border and brought the rebels to battle in what became labelled as the 'Leicester war' on marshy land by the River Lark at Fornham St Genevieve, only some two miles north of St Edmund's Abbey.

Abbey knights and local countrymen of all types played a very big part not only in this defeat of Leicester's Flemings but also in bringing to heel Hugh Bigod and his supporters. Having capitulated and been captured, some of the same rebels renewed their efforts later, encouraged by Louis of France, but Henry was a very active and mobile King and, although attempts to deprive him of some of his lands in England and on the continent, particularly in Aquitaine, continued to spring up like bush fires, they were all quelled and enemy castles destroyed. Henry's castles were repaired and strengthened. The death of King Louis of France in September

---

[1] All the first four Earls of Leicester were called Robert: this was the 3rd Earl.

1180 meant the end of much of the disruption. But when Samson and a supporting monk Ruffus visited the King on the continent to report Abbot Hugh's death a few months later, it is understandable that King Henry's attention was more focused on the impact of the death of an old enemy in France, in particular on Aquitaine, than on that of an ineffective Abbot in Bury St Edmunds. This was a situation which Samson, the opportunist, almost certainly would have exploited. The last thing that an ambitious and individualistic sub-sacrist would have welcomed would have been the promotion to Abbot of Prior Robert, at a time when otherwise Samson could see little to hold back his own career.

Samson's reporting of the situation at the Abbey, therefore, would certainly have been a recognition of all the matters of great moment to the nation confronting the King at the time together with strongly confident reassurances that he, Samson, had all the necessary building and repair work in hand, that all the other officers were properly fulfilling their task and that the Prior was accustomed to deputising for the Abbot. In short, that the appointment of a new Abbot could certainly wait upon the time that could be spared when affairs of state were less pressing: a course which King Henry would have been unlikely to resist. So the dead man's shoes remained empty and for the next two years the Abbey at Bury St Edmunds continued on a path of laissez-faire – the Prior, Robert, letting each go his own way; William, the sacrist, spending far beyond the Abbey's means on the inconsequential, yet failing to pay debts or maintain the essential; the cellarer allowing lavish entertainment in the Abbey and pleasing the monks with his spending on domestic catering. Samson, by his rather obvious conscientiousness and strict observance of budgetary care was the exception, and unpopular as a result. Various attempts were made by some of the other monks to discredit him, but he survived.

Quite apart from the increasing weight of debt on the Abbey, particularly to Jewish money-lenders, there was no doubt that the influence of St Edmund's Abbey had ebbed away since Abbot Anselm's death. It had certainly become unworthy as the site of St Edmund's shrine and this was particularly unfortunate as it coincided with the canonisation of Thomas Becket as a result of his murder at Canterbury. The cathedral there, the shrine of the new saint, rapidly began to replace St Edmund's Abbey as the main place of pilgrimage in England and Henry II's conscience about the murder ensured that when he was in England there were several penitential visits to Canterbury, which felt the King's favour more than Bury St Edmunds in consequence.

CHAPTER 4

'The Time has Come'

The play which had been set up by Samson, the sub-sacrist, in 1180 on his visit to King Henry II, moved inexorably into its second act in 1182. The King ordered that the Prior and twelve members of the convent should appear before him on a nominated day to elect an Abbot. Prior Robert nominated from the south (Abbot's) side of the monks' choir six candidates, including the sub-sacrist and the 'third' Prior (Hugh – the next in line after the sub-Prior). From his side of the choir the Prior nominated the balance, including William, the sacrist, Roger, the cellarer, and Master Walter, the physician.

This idea of thirteen candidates attending on the King to make the choice of an Abbot was a new approach which inevitably provoked much discussion at the Abbey. The appointment of a new Abbot was the King's prerogative, and where he had personal knowledge of possible candidates, he would normally do this without any selection procedure. Alternatively he could leave it to the convent to elect their own.

The twelve candidates, considering how the selection would work out in practice, were concerned that disagreement between them in front of the King would reflect badly on the Abbey, so some were in favour of an election amongst themselves so that one candidate could be put forward to the King. However, they felt that this could be considered by the King as presumptuous. It was again the sub-sacrist, Samson, who took the lead, proposing that six should be elected by the convent comprising four 'confessors'[1] and two of the most senior monks, and these six should select the three men best qualified under the Benedictine Rule to serve as Abbot. The names of these would be taken in a sealed document by those attending on the King and if the King appeared to be prepared to allow this new Abbot to be selected from the convent, the three names could be revealed. If, however, he was not, the seal would remain unbroken and no one's reputation would be damaged.

Once again, during the working through of the system, it was Samson who was in the forefront. It was he who put forward that all the candidates should 'take a solemn oath that whoever is elected will treat the convent reasonably, not changing the chief obedientiaries[2] without the consent of the convent, nor putting an excessive burden on the sacrist, nor making anyone a monk without the convent's permission.' Later, also at Samson's suggestion, it was proposed that whoever became Abbot should have sworn

---

[1] Ordained monks.
[2] Abbey officials.

to restore the churches in the convent's diocese to the hospitality fund. All the monks agreed to both these proposals except the Prior, who argued, reasonably enough, that any Abbot committed to so many sworn oaths would shrink from attempting the task.

The King received the delegation on 21st February 1182 with Richard, Bishop of Winchester and Geoffrey Plantagenet the Royal Chancellor. He called for three nominations from the Abbey. Those named in the sealed package were put forward: Hugh, the third Prior, Roger the cellarer and Samson the sub-sacrist. The King then called for a further three candidates from the convent to be nominated which led to the Prior himself, William the sacrist, and Master Denis[3] being put forward. Finally, in the interests of other convents within his realm, the King asked for nominations from other monasteries.

After a whittling down of these nine names (the first to go being those from other monasteries) only Robert the Prior and Samson were being considered. Brother Denis became spokesman for the Abbey and, though praising them both, produced the firm impression that the Prior would be too easy-going whereas Samson would be strict, hard-working, efficient in secular affairs and had already proved himself capable of accepting considerable responsibility. Samson was duly elected.

Samson was very much an East Anglian countryman. He was born in the small village of Tottington in the Breckland, north

---

[3] Some monastery officals who were monks had the title 'master'. See Glossary.

of Thetford, probably in 1135. He lost his father at an early age and seems to have owed his education to one William of Diss who had a school there on the Norfolk/Suffolk border. The dialect that would have surrounded him would have been that of Norfolk and Samson continued to be able to use this when appropriate throughout his life. He was clearly a very bright boy who worked hard to improve his circumstances. With help from friends he managed to continue his education in Paris and seems to have had a natural facility for learning languages as well as acquiring social graces. He returned to England probably in 1159 or 1160 and was employed at the Bury St Edmunds school where he got to know the Prior and monks at the Abbey.

Because of his superior education and facility for languages, not to mention his already evident spirit of adventure, Samson undertook a difficult mission to Rome on the Abbey's behalf. This he carried out successfully in spite of numerous hazards on the way: a success which endeared him to the Prior and monks but – it seems probably because of this – incurred the dislike of the unpredictable Abbot, Hugh. Thus, when Samson became a monk at the Abbey in 1166, he was often the subject of Hugh's draconian punishments, usually as a result of his forthright attitude and refusal to say always the right or emollient phrases to the Abbot. Consequently he was more than once 'rusticated' by Abbot Hugh to Castle Acre Priory, some twenty miles north into Norfolk where, no doubt, Hugh would have preferred Samson to remain – particularly when the latter was raising awkward questions about the administration and discipline at Bury.

Once again the St Edmundsbury Abbey had an Abbot qualified to raise it to the standard previously maintained by first Baldwin and then Anselm. Samson had not the classical background of these two predecessors, nor their depth of spirituality but he was well-educated (for the period), determined and experienced in the ways of the world. He also had, as a very high priority, a firm resolve to honour St Edmund and to restore the site of his shrine to its rightful place as a focus of pilgrimage in England. He had genuine belief in himself as the specially chosen disciple of Edmund, promoter of his supernatural powers and upholder of full reverence for his relics. He contributed to the first book on the miracles of St Edmund.

He was also a very practical man with strong convictions and understanding of the secular world. He had sound commercial sense (which was just as well at the time of his appointment to the abbacy). He could be ruthless and tended to view life in black and white, ignoring the possibility of there being shades of either.

These two sides of Samson's character were quickly illustrated by two of his early acts. He made the earliest possible settlement of the numerous debts of the Abbey his first secular care, and he dismissed his previous master, William the sacrist, who had allowed the Abbey virtually to fall into the hands of Jewish money-lenders. The total debt of the Abbey would be the equivalent of at least £500,000 in this century. Samson made sure that every debt was declared in detail and he identified, by personal visits, all the sources of income from the Abbey's estates, farms, manors and town property. It was a gradual process but by rapid practical action he removed the hold which the usurers had acquired over the Abbey and its people, including the destruction of no fewer than thirty-two convent seals which had been used by individuals to authenticate the loans they had procured, allegedly on behalf of the Abbey.

An important part of Samson's character was his political skill. Perhaps it was an educated development of a countryman's innate cunning. There were early signs of this on his errand for the Abbey before he was even a monk. He visited Pope Alexander II in order to obtain for the Abbey rights over the church and benefice of Woolpit, about which there had been considerable controversy. A journey to Rome in the mid-12th century was hazardous in any event. One Octavian, a strong anti-Alexander contender as Pope, was supported by the German Emperor, and any messenger visiting Alexander was liable to attack on the European mainland, and, if caught, was subject to imprisonment, hanging or, for some, the 'cutting off of lips and noses' and being sent to Alexander 'to his disgrace and confusion'. Samson, when he appeared to be threatened, pretended to be a Scot, Scotland being a supporter of Octavian. On his way back to England, having obtained the Pope's writ concerning Woolpit, Samson was stopped and searched at a castle but by sleight of hand succeeded in concealing the writ. He lost his belongings and his money in the search and had to beg for the rest of his journey home. He appears merely to have considered himself fortunate not to have had any worse experience and to have been under the protection of the Almighty and St Edmund.

There is little doubt that Samson's visit to Rome helped him to a favoured position in Pope Alexander's eyes and his handling of the interregnum at the Abbey on his visit to King Henry and his subsequent performance before the King at his election to Abbot gave Samson a very good start with Henry II. His strong grip on the Abbey's affairs and evident moves to rebuild the reputation of St Edmund's shrine soon impressed both the King and the Pope. Samson had been Abbot for less than a year when the then Pope, Lucius III, appointed him a judge in the church courts and he subsequently headed various church commissions into disputed matters.

With his important patrons firmly behind him and the Abbey's debts being properly serviced and diminished, Samson's abundant energy was more fully directed towards the people of the Abbey's rural possessions and the townspeople of Bury St Edmunds. Samson's strong character and evident virility had favourably impressed those with whom he had come into contact when sorting out the Abbey's estates and manors, and his ability to converse in the vernacular, as well as French and Latin, made it easy for him to associate with both the peasant and knightly population equally well. He installed a pulpit in the church and preached there quite frequently using the dialect understood by his fellow East Anglians. As time went by the improvement in the Abbey finances enabled him to continue, at last, the completion of the western tower of the Abbey and some of the small interior chapels. He built a new almonry and infirmary and added adornments to the shrine.

The very aspects of the new Abbot's character which so commended themselves to peasants and nobles alike – his straightforward, thrustful attitude and uncompromising opinions – meant that his relations with some of the more contemplative and more unworldly monks and churchmen was difficult. He found easy agreement with those doing official tasks within the Abbey and with the many involved in secular work but seemed to have little time for those monks concentrating on their devotions. Indeed, at one point, Samson had to make it clear to the convent that he was accessible to all the members, there had been such an apparent barrier developing between those who ideally should have a relationship approaching that of father and sons.

Samson's attitude to the Jewish community in Bury St Edmunds had from the first been one of contempt for their usury and hostility for their continuing alien ways in spite of their lengthy residence in England. He regarded the capture of Jerusalem by Saladin in 1187 as a major tragedy for Christendom – almost a repetition of Good Friday. He dressed in hair-cloth breeches and a hair shirt and abstained from meat, and in Chapter he took to railing against the Jews and encouraging preaching to the townspeople condemnation of the beliefs and way of life of these 'anti-Christians'. He equated the Jews with the Saracens as equal enemies of Christ and reminded the Chapter of the deaths of two Christian children, William of Norwich and Robert of Bury, whose murders had been alleged to have been ritual killings by Jews. To the protests of those who remembered the Bible teaching that God's will was that the Jews should be scattered not killed, and that the crucifixion was part of the Almighty's plan, not something that He could neither predict or prevent, Samson responded roughly that since the events of Good Friday the Jews had shown themselves to be more and more anti-Christ and by their greed had done their best to destroy Christian communities. He revealed that when King Henry II visited the Abbey to pray, on deciding to 'take the cross' on the Third Crusade, their Abbot had asked the King's permission to do the same. In the event King Henry's illness prevented his participation and the Bishop of Norwich had seen to it that Samson was denied permission.

The Prior and sub-Prior would undoubtedly have tried to calm the atmosphere by pointing out that Jews were already barred from the Abbey precincts, and now were bereft of the power they had held through their money-lending to the Abbey and its members. They were also likely, as tactfully as possible, to have reminded the Abbot that there was already a very intense distrust and hatred of the Jews amongst the more uneducated, and violent, sector of the population which was unreasoning, and that any incitement from the Abbey could quickly lead to extremely unchristian violence in the pattern already seen on the continent. There was a risk of the Jews being portrayed as less than human and if this happened all excesses might be considered acceptable.

Just after this meeting the death of Henry II cast a gloom over the whole country and there was a feeling of dread that there would be a return to the anarchy of the days of Queen Matilda and King Stephen, because of the competition for power and land between Queen Eleanor's surviving sons, Richard,

Geoffrey Plantagenet and John. The two powerful sponsors previously involved in this rivalry for inheritance had been King Philip Augustus of France and Queen Eleanor, Henry II's widow. The latter, though, had been immobilized for some time, having been imprisoned by her husband, and Philip put all his support behind Richard.

Richard, Duke of Aquitaine, was invested as Duke of Normandy at Rouen in July 1189 and in September was anointed King Richard I in Westminster Abbey by Baldwin, Archbishop of Canterbury. One of his first acts after his father's death had been to order the release from imprisonment of his mother, Queen Eleanor, and she had already gone about ensuring support for Richard amongst the most powerful men in England, some of whom had previously supported her erstwhile favoured candidate, John.

The face of England at this time was more unclouded than for many years. Richard was looking secure on his throne, and his mother, once again enjoying the exercise of charm and power on the continent as well as in England and this time by courtesy of Richard, appeared to have abandoned upward pressure on her favourite, John. Against this background the Abbey of St Edmund also prospered. Its administration was efficient; it was quite clear of debt, indeed it was the fourth richest monastery in England; its Abbot was respected by both Pope and King and was of very high standing in both legal and noble fields. His strong line with Jews and often expressed support for the Third Crusade, as well as his generally masterful aspect, were popular with tenants and countrymen alike. It was only within the Abbey that there were many who regretted the increasing secularity which Samson had brought with him, and looked back wistfully to the days of Anselm and Hugo, when spirituality characterized the Abbey in its liturgy, its art and its everyday life.

CHAPTER 5

'Of Kings'

The development of a firm friendship between Abbot Samson and King Richard I seems, at first sight, to be somewhat surprising. Seemingly they had little in common. Richard, a tall, strong and handsome offspring of the great Angevin line, was a distinguished soldier brought up in the company of earls and barons and almost entirely in continental Europe. Samson, according to his contemporary biographer, Jocelin, was:

> 'of medium height and almost completely bald. His face was neither round nor long, and he had a prominent nose and thick lips. ... His eyebrows were bushy, and were frequently trimmed.'

Clearly he was rather unprepossessing, very much a provincial lad, educated locally at first, although subsequently in Paris, where he had acquired a liberal education by hard work and a lively intelligence. With this had come great self-confidence – and a degree of arrogance. This latter characteristic was one which he shared with Richard (though the King was more often able to display his) together with impetuosity and ruthlessness. Perhaps the element in Samson's nature which Richard most appreciated was his predilection for soldiering. It seems likely, too, that Richard found this down-to-earth, almost materialistic Abbot rather easier to understand than he would, say, an Anselm.

Both men had had to fight their way up, though in different ways: Richard against the competition of his father, and his brothers, and to convert empty honours into reality; Samson to raise himself above his original environment and then to overcome the disapproval of his Abbot. So although on the surface there was not much common ground, they found each other to be congenial company whenever their paths crossed.

It was probably part of King Richard's impetuosity that he could rarely bother with assembling a large court when he travelled. He arrived at Bury St Edmunds on the eve of St Edmund's festival in November 1189 with only his chaplain and a small escort.

Samson, the author of a book on the miracles attributed to St Edmund, would have found Richard a willing listener and one who needed no persuading that Edmund was truly a soldier's saint. The King's devotions at St Edmund's shrine and the very great respect in which he clearly held the saint could not fail to endear him to the Abbot. On the other side, the obvious interest that Samson had in military affairs, particularly in the crusades, and the fact that he had indeed volunteered to accompany King

Henry in the Second Crusade, must have helped to ensure that he and his Abbey both stood high in King Richard's esteem.

After their devotions at the shrine, it was certain that Hugo's cross, on the altar in the monks' choir, would have come to Richard's attention. The skill and artistry of the carving and the detail of its scenes and inscriptions could not have failed to grip the imagination of a king of Richard's temperament. The hard-hitting nature of some of the messages of the cross (which were unlikely to have been played down by Samson) would have had a special appeal to Richard, who was as willing as the Abbot to consider crusades as being directed against all non-Christians.

The King, a veteran of campaigning, would have especially admired the compactness of the cross and the ingenuity which enabled the relatively small tusks to be brought together in the cross and, as easily, taken apart. The value of such an inspiring artefact to crusaders is likely also to have impressed the King's chaplain, and all who saw it at that time must have been struck by its potential significance to the army of the Third Crusade, and to the Templars in particular, if the cross which they 'took' could indeed be exemplified by such a unique Christian artefact which came from the very shrine of a soldier-king.

It was very much contrary to Samson's nature to avoid personal responsibility; to defer a decision for necessary consultation, but even he would have hesitated to agree to part with an Abbey treasure without involving the Chapter. He may have postponed the reaction by an immediate offer – by no means ill-considered – to accompany the King on the crusade himself (a repeat of his application to Henry). This could only have been met with a kindly rebuff as before, on the grounds of Samson's great value at such an important establishment; particularly important to the stability of the homeland while the Sovereign was abroad, and important to the ecclesiastical hierarchy. It would have been surprising, however, if the King had not found the offer an irresistible opportunity to describe the provision of the cross as a very worthy and appropriate substitute for the Abbot himself and his support.

There is little doubt that, for Samson, the goodwill of King Richard and the ability to provide valuable support for the crusade, would more than have outweighed the value of the cross as an asset for the Abbey. For him, the presence of King Edmund's shrine and relics was everything. An artefact, however brilliantly conceived and executed, was valuable only for what it achieved, and, as matters stood in Bury St Edmunds, the cross was seen only by those who knew it well and by other believers. No longer could he feel that it was an evangelistic instrument. In the world outside, and very specifically in Outremer, Samson believed that the cross would once again exert its power. It is likely that the King would have been confident that when he embarked with his crusaders the Hugo cross would accompany him – and so it transpired.

That the impressive forces promised to the Third Crusade by the Emperor of Germany, the King of Sicily, King Philip Augustus of France and King Richard of England were still nowhere near their enemy, Saladin, by the early spring of 1191, was a disgrace

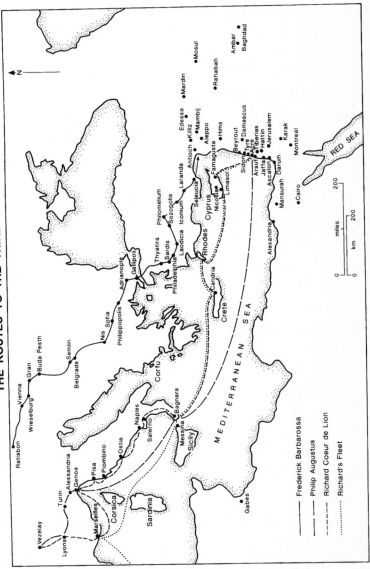

THE ROUTES TO THE THIRD CRUSADE

as far as the exhausted besieging crusaders of Acre were concerned, but was a fair reflection of the internal disruption of Europe in this part of the 12th century. The first to set off was Emperor Frederick 'Barbarossa' of Germany, who left Ratisbon (Regensburg) in Eastern Germany with the plan of reaching Palestine by land through the Balkans and Byzantium. It was astride the Bosphorus that, having been attacked on all sides for much of the latter part of their journey, the greater part of Frederick's army perished in June 1190, though a remnant, possibly only 1000, of the original 30–40,000 eventually reached Acre in August of that year. Frederick himself had drowned, which further diminished the value of the German contribution.

King Philip Augustus of France assembled his force at Paris and then went to a rendezvous with Richard at Vezelay in Burgundy on 11th July 1190, where they agreed upon a division of the 'spoils' of the crusade on which they had yet to embark. The two kings travelled together to Lyons where they separated: Philip to join his troops at Genoa and Richard to his embarkation port of Marseille. Philip became ill at Genoa but used his time there to establish good relations with Tancred, the recently installed King of Sicily, the next stage on the way to Palestine. In this way the French contingent of some 6–7000 knights and infantry received a welcome at Messina in contrast to the Sicilian attitude to Richard.

The Sicilian throne should have passed to Henry VI of Saxony who was married to the previous king's aunt, Constance of Sicily. The rejection of a German king carried with it enmity also to

Richard, whose sister Joan had been the wife of the late King of Sicily. Philip Augustus had lost no opportunity to aggravate this animosity against Richard, partly in line with his continuing chipping away at Richard's lands on the mainland, and partly because Richard was not honouring his childhood betrothal to Philip's sister, Alice. Thus Richard's arrival in Sicily was greeted by his sister Joan being imprisoned and money inherited from her husband being denied to Richard.

Part of Richard's crusading force had left Marseille for Syria directly under Baldwin, the Archbishop of Canterbury, Hubert Walter, Bishop of Salisbury and Ranulf Glanville, and they arrived at Tyre on 16th September and reached Acre on 12th October. Meanwhile, the bulk of the French and British forces spent the winter in Sicily building up money and supplies but also thoroughly bad relationships. King Richard was at his most arrogant and, provoked by the Sicilian attitude, set his men to capture Messina. Tancred decided that he would rather have Richard on his side than Philip, so negotiated a treaty with the former including offering him twenty thousand ounces of gold, with a similar sum for his sister, the recently imprisoned Joan.

In the strange way of the times, when yesterday's greatest enemy became today's dinner companion, Kings Philip and Richard now reached agreement on all the details for the administration and conduct of the crusade and Philip even accepted that Richard's marriage to sister Alice would never take place.

It was on 10th April 1191 when King Richard eventually set sail across the Mediterranean. The exodus from England of a newly crowned king, his most trusted bishops, barons, knights and supporters, leaving behind his ambitious brother John and those who might benefit from the latter's rule, would seem to have been taking unjustified risks with England's recently acquired, but still rather fragile, stability. That anarchy did not return was partly attributable to the influence of Queen Eleanor, the Queen Mother, but also to Henry II's foresight and planning in establishing his authority over the remaining rebels and in setting up sound administrative and judicial systems and ensuring that the country's finances were prudently managed.

His Chancellor, Thomas Becket, had always been a loyal supporter of the House of Anjou against Stephen and, under the Chancellor, Henry had appointed two justiciars: men of substance who were the chief administrators of justice and government for their respective areas. For these important posts he chose two men who had previously been supporters of King Stephen against the House of Anjou; but he chose them for their character and intelligence. They were Robert Beaumont, Earl of Leicester and Richard de Lucy, and they served him well.

There was a period when conflict between Crown and Church appeared to threaten Henry's firm control once again, as a result of Becket's appointment to be Archbishop of Canterbury, his resignation as Chancellor and his subsequent quarrel with Henry, culminating in Becket's murder at Canterbury. Henry's system held, however, assisted with some good fortune in the way of the elimination of several of his prominent malcontents through natural causes, and he was able to ensure that replacements for these came from his supporters. One of these was William Longchamp who became King Richard's Chancellor and Bishop of Ely: an appointment which was to have repercussions both on the life of the nation and on local affairs at Bury St Edmunds.

Longchamp was a complete contrast to the type of person previously selected to act for the Crown in England. Robert Beaumont, Richard de Lucy, and their successors as justiciars Ranulf Glanville, Hugh de Puiset and William de Mandeville came from the higher strata of Norman and English society, while Longchamp came from humble stock.

He was also unprepossessing to a degree; he was short and bent (likened by one of his contemporaries to an ape) and ugly of countenance. His ambition was boundless and perhaps his upstart nature and consciousness of his personal appearance made him the more ruthless; particularly in his attitude to the native English and their customs. It may have been his contempt for England that made his compatibility with King Richard understandable, which otherwise would have seemed so strange.

Longchamp's earliest acts after Richard's departure were directed to establishing a virtual dictatorship in his role as regent. He arranged the arrest of Hugh de Puiset, the Bishop of Durham (and his fellow justiciar), by Longchamp's brother Osbert whom he had installed as Sheriff in Yorkshire. In 1190 he was appointed Papal Legate and he set about bringing the Church to heel by making visitations to religious establishments which were punishing both in their treatment and in their demands of hospitality. Like most bullies, however, he usually backed down if opposed in a determined fashion, and he met his match in Abbot Samson of Bury St Edmunds who refused his visits and ignored his decrees.

Longchamp's behaviour made him so disliked in England that people were even beginning to wish for rule by John, and by 1192 he had made so many enemies that he had to leave the country. However, he remained loyal to Richard and, as will be seen, was trusted by him in times of danger.

At the end of it all, though, the combination of Henry II's structure for administering England, Queen Eleanor's continuing grip on the nation's affairs, once released from imprisonment, and the balance of forces and their loyalties in England, kept a degree of stability as long as the eventual return of Richard was assured.

CHAPTER 6

'We've Brought Them Out so Far'

Before following King Richard's voyage from Messina on his way to the Holy Land, it is very relevant to assess the situation there. The two most important figures among the Franks were Guy of Lusignan, King of Jerusalem in title rather than fact, and his rival, Conrad, Marquis of Montferrat.

The failure of the Second Crusade in 1148 to establish the Franks as the masters of Outremer, and the resurgence of the Muslim forces under Saladin, meant that the Franks became more and more outnumbered for a generation, and that their sovereignty was restricted to certain strongholds – largely along the coast and high ground. When Saladin captured Tiberias in 1187, Guy of Lusignan was camped some twenty kilometres to the east. Although aware that an attack by his relatively small Latin army across waterless desert would put his whole army at risk in conditions which suited the Saracens, Guy moved to relieve Tiberias. The Franks were caught on the march by Saladin's men at a place called Hattin and in two days they were virtually destroyed as an organised fighting force. In the same year the Turks were in possession of Acre and at the time of the Third Crusade, Guy, with 700 knights and about 9,000 men, was investing the town and castle.

Conrad had a more successful record against Saladin. He was in command at Tyre and had resisted all Saladin's efforts to capture it in 1187. Tyre and Acre were the only ports in Palestine still open to shipping from the West in 1190, but the situation in Acre was tense, with the town and castle still occupied by the Turks but closely besieged by Guy de Lusignan's forces who, in turn, were almost encircled by large numbers of Turks. It was a situation in which both besiegers and besieged were suffering from hunger, thirst and disease.

There can be little doubt that the new forces of the Third Crusade were eagerly awaited in Palestine.

There were three routes by which the crusading reinforcements could move into Palestine to recover the land captured by Saladin: either through Asia Minor and thence to Antioch in the north, or by sea to the Mediterranean coast in the west, or up from the Nile delta in the south. The northern land route had been that chosen by Frederick 'Barbarossa' and his German crusaders and their fate in Byzantium has already been described. The southerly route from Egypt would remain impracticable as long as the Saracens held Ascalon and, therefore, the approaches in the Gaza–Hebron area. The sea route across the Mediterranean remained the most favourable, particularly as long as Tyre was a Frankish port, and re-supply and reinforcement by shipping was always available with any Saracen vessels being usually much inferior in size and numbers to those from the North.

Acre, which had been held by Guy of Lusignan and had fallen to Saladin in 1187, was of great importance to the Franks and the Crusaders as both a port and a base. As a port it was much closer to the Christian centre and goal, Jerusalem, than the northern ports of Beyrout, Sidon and Tyre, and it had good approaches to Jerusalem along the coastal plain.

The town possessed a strong castle and had been a base for both the Knights Templar and Hospitallers. There was an outer and inner harbour, but the inner was close up under the city walls and vulnerable to sorties from there; the outer, while more secure from attack from the land, provided only a limited protection against wind and weather from the west and south, because the city was built on a small promontory, the headland of which faced south, and the protecting reef was low and only effective against moderate seas.

As soon as King Guy had assembled what he considered to be a large enough force to lay siege to Acre in August 1189 he took up a position surrounding the city at close range on the landward side to the north and east. Crusaders from Pisa came by sea and completed the ring of besiegers on the sea shore. Before Guy's forces could make any worthwhile break in the Saracen's defences, though, Saladin had managed to throw an encircling ring round the besiegers on the land side.

So it was that 1190 saw the Franks and Crusaders able to

reinforce only from the sea and the Saracens more easily capable of building up on the land; only those besieged were isolated.

In spite of its limitations as a port, the reason for the struggle for Acre is patent, and both sides concentrated on reinforcing throughout 1190 (even Conrad was persuaded to join the siege with around 1,000 knights and 20,000 men). Although the crusaders succeeded in controlling the harbour, the stalemate continued and the additional numbers involved accentuated the sufferings from famine and disease: circumstances in which tension and rivalry between commanders and differing races (although, in theory, on the same side) flourished. Clearly there was a crying need for an inspiring leader and a good military brain to end the deadlock at Acre.

Philip Augustus of France, at the head of the French crusaders, sailed from Messina on 30th March 1191 with Hugh, Duke of Burgundy, and Philip, Count of Flanders. They disembarked at Tyre where they were met by Conrad, who was Philip's cousin, and arrived at Acre on 20th April, where they reinforced Conrad's existing force. No attempt was made then to mount an assault on Acre. This awaited Richard's arrival and he was otherwise engaged.

He had left Messina with a fleet of about 200 ships. His party now included his sister, Joan, chaperoning his bride-to-be, Princess Berengaria, daughter of King Sancho of Navarre, Richard having disengaged himself from the French Princess Alice at the cost of 10,000 marks and some 'slight territorial adjustments' to his lands in France. Richard's fleet was badly dispersed in strong winds. His own ship sheltered for a day at Crete and then had a very rough passage to Rhodes where Richard stayed until 1st May recovering from *mal de mer*. One of his ships foundered in the storm and another three were driven on to Cyprus. Two were wrecked, but the vessel carrying Joan and Berengaria anchored safely at Limassol.

The Cypriot ruler, who styled himself 'Emperor', Isaac Comnenus, was immediately hostile. His own position was unpopular and insecure and he hated 'Franks', largely because he feared them. His immediate reaction to the arrival of Richard's ships was to arrest the crews and confiscate any salvaged goods. He invited Queen Joan and Princess Berengaria to land, but the former knew about hostage-taking and responded that without King Richard's permission this was not possible. Isaac refused any supply of fresh water to the ship and set about fortifying Limassol against the possibility of any further English landings.

Richard's main fleet did not complete its passage from Rhodes until a week later. It had been a very stormy journey, Richard's ship had been near to destruction just off the Turkish coast. He was a bad sailor and already in a belligerent mood before he heard of the treatment meted out to his sister and his betrothed. The result was a foregone conclusion. A King Richard with a thoroughly unpleasant voyage just completed and his *amour-propre* damaged was not likely to pay a courtesy call on Isaac Comnenus. He landed his troops near Limassol and marched on the town. Quite apart from the unpopularity of Isaac, most of the local people of substance, who were 'Franks' themselves, welcomed Richard. Isaac, (generally from a safe distance) attempted to bluff and bargain but when Richard's party was joined by a ship full of crusaders from Acre led by King Guy, his brother, Geoffrey, and other leaders who had come to gain Richard's early support against the Conrad supporters, Isaac began a full retreat.

Richard and the visitors from Palestine clearly saw the advantage of Cyprus, both as a supply base for the crusade and as a guarantee against it providing a support for Saladin, and Richard decided on its conquest. First, however, there was a royal wedding at St George's Chapel in Limassol, where King Richard married Princess Berengaria, who was crowned Queen of England by the Bishop of Evreux. Against little opposition Richard's army, latterly under King Guy's command because Richard became ill in Nicosia, occupied Cyprus and Isaac surrendered unconditionally. King Richard despatched the captured standard of the Cypriot Emperor to St Edmund's Abbey, perhaps as a part exchange for the cross, and such a trophy would certainly have been appreciated by Abbot Samson even if regarded as an irrelevance by very many. The crusaders benefited from an enormous amount of booty, Frankish garrisons were established in the many castles on the island and two English justiciars were appointed to administer the island. It was a conquest destined to last for a very long time.

On 5th June 1191 King Richard and a substantial part of his expeditionary force set sail for the Holy Land. It was a fair reflection of the relationship between Richard and his supporters, including King Guy of Jerusalem on the one hand, and Philip

Augustus of France and his allies, including Conrad of Tyre, on the other, that King Richard's fleet (which included Guy) was refused access to his nearest landfall at Tyre and so continued southwards to Acre itself. On June 7th during the voyage to Acre Richard's fleet encountered a very large Saracen galley which tried to pass itself off as belonging to Philip of France. When Richard challenged this, the Saracens made to attack. King Richard may not have been much of a sailor but he had ample confidence that his northern ships were much superior vessels to the Saracen galleys and he ordered that the Saracens should be rammed. This was entirely successful: the Saracen ship was sunk and many prisoners taken. It was a good preamble to Richard's arrival at Acre.

Richard found a dispirited besieging force at Acre, where relief and expectation at his arrival on the 8th June were demonstrated by trumpets and bonfires. There were some useful siege weapons in the crusaders' armoury already deployed which had been battering at the walls of Acre for some time, but there had been no forceful military leader with both the skill and charisma to put new life into the weary, and none too healthy, soldiers. Richard's reputation and manifest self-confidence invigorated everyone – including even his jealous detractors. An early example of this self-confidence was his approach, through an intermediary, to Saladin, suggesting a meeting. Saladin countered with an offer for his brother to meet Richard during a short truce – a meeting which never took place because both Richard and Philip became ill with a fever which had long debilitated the

Frankish besiegers.[1] Nevertheless Richard kept up both the bombardments and the crusaders' spirits, and small breaches in the defences were achieved.

These, though, were never big enough to make a major assault, and during the whole of this period Saladin's troops encircling the crusaders on the land side were being strengthened by the influx of tribesmen from Mesopotamia and Egypt so that the besiegers were themselves being besieged on all but the sea side. Fortunately the sea was controlled by the crusaders' ships and there were consequently few problems of reinforcement and re-supply.

Nevertheless the quarrelsome atmosphere, which had bedevilled the command and control of the crusaders for so long, remained. The rivals for the throne of Jerusalem still being occupied by Saladin's forces, even though virtually only a throne 'in exile', would not relax their squabbling and their supporters divided the Frankish forces. The result was that a properly co-ordinated attack by the crusaders which could have brought an early end to Saladin's garrison never took place. In the end, after a failure by Saladin's nephew to reach and reinforce the garrison, Philip's Frenchmen succeeded in breaking through but were driven back. Richard's men followed this up and although they did not capture the town,

---

[1] Among the possible candidates for this disease must have been scurvy, since some of the symptoms are similar to those described (although loss of hair tends to point to syphilis which may well have been present in some): but it seems certain that, in addition to dietary deficiencies, the Crusaders would have fallen victims to infection, both directly from bad hygiene and indirectly from mosquito bites leading to malaria or yellow fever.

the garrison had had enough. A last appeal was made by the desperate Saracens to Saladin but his troops, too, were weary and beyond mounting a really big rescue operation at short notice. The garrison sued for peace and surrendered on 12th July.

The terms for their capitulation, which Saladin felt bound to honour, were:

- The surrender of Acre with all its contents, its ships and military stores and equipment
- 200 gold pieces for the Crusaders with an additional 400 to Conrad
- All 1,500 named Christian prisoners to be liberated
- The True Cross to be restored

In return, the lives of the garrison were to be spared.

The surrender terms are simple to record; to implement them was less so and King Richard who, with Philip returned to France, was now in overall command of the crusaders, was not a patient man when engagement in battle was concerned.

Saladin was an honourable man and undoubtedly did his best to assemble all the Christian prisoners and to find the money. The first was clearly a lengthy process and three weeks after Acre had capitulated a delegation from Richard brought his acceptance to Saladin that the return of Christian prisoners and the money payment could occur at three-monthly intervals. The Saracen prisoners would be freed by the crusaders once the first instalment had been received.

The first batch and payment were received on 11th August but Richard's envoys protested that although the total numbers of freed prisoners were correct, the most important, who had been nominated by the crusaders, were not all included. The Saracen prisoners would not be freed until this omission had been rectified. Saladin made an offer to provide hostages as a guarantee of eventually returning all the Christian prisoners if the Saracen prisoners were released to him, or to provide hostages with Saladin until they were. Richard's representatives would not agree to either proposal and would only promise that if the specified prisoners were released by Saladin then the Saracen captives would be freed. It was a bargaining process that led only to greater distrust on both sides and a deadlock ensued: a situation which simply could not be permitted to exist by a King Richard literally on the warpath. He pronounced Saladin's action as having broken the terms of the agreement and he ordered the execution of all the Saracen prisoners.

One of those who had 'held the fort' for King Richard while the latter was pursuing other interests in Sicily and Cyprus was Hubert Walter, Bishop of Salisbury. His military skill and leadership had stood out during the long period of stalemate at Acre and, although he willingly transferred the overall command of the English forces to the King on his arrival, he continued to distinguish himself in the fighting and was prominent in the final assault. On more than one occasion during Richard's bouts of illness it was Hubert who assumed command.

The action by Richard in beheading the almost 3,000 members

of the Acre garrison because Saladin had not yet fulfilled his commitments to provide the money and the True Cross, must have been difficult for Bishop Hubert to swallow. Saladin, who had always been meticulous in honouring truces and other agreements, reacted by returning the True Cross to Damascus. He did not execute the Frankish prisoners he held, but he forswore the taking of Frankish prisoners in the future. This savage, and apparently unwarranted, action by Richard seemed to have no great emotion of fanaticism behind it: simply the military argument that the crusaders could not afford to delay any longer in this unhealthy place, they could not take nearly 3,000 prisoners with them, and leaving such a force of hardened soldiers behind at Acre without an adequate garrison to keep them secure, and fed, was not sensible. Also in the background was Pope Urban II's call to arms to rescue Jerusalem from the hands of infidels. To all who took part he offered remission of the sin of killing an infidel. In the words of St Bernard, 'The Knight of Christ need fear no sin in killing the foe. He is the minister of God for the punishment of the wicked. In the death of a pagan a Christian is glorified because Christ is glorified.' So the presence of the ivory cross would not necessarily have been a deterrent to the executions; indeed at times like this the anti-heathen aspects of the cross may have done much to strengthen the crusaders' resolve.

Richard lost no time. His plan was to march parallel to the coast so that his right flank was secure. Only some five weeks after the surrender of Acre, Richard set out from there. Philip of

FIELDS OF BATTLE IN 'OUTREMER'

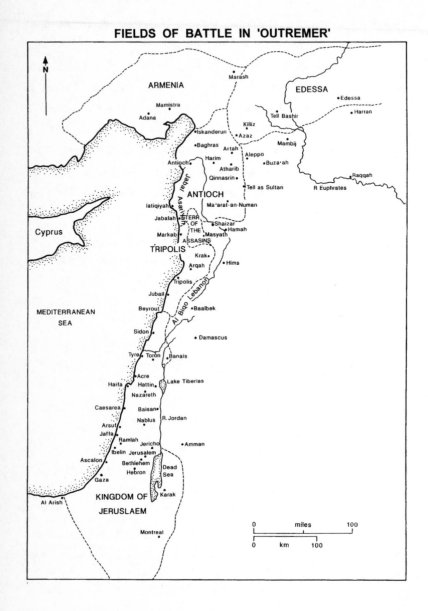

France, unwell and anxious about affairs at home, had left for France, and the Duke of Burgundy and the French crusaders fell in behind Richard's men where, tending to lag behind, they suffered greatly from the attacks by Saladin's Turkish horsemen, whose tactic was always to harry the flanks and rear of columns. Richard's response to these sharp flank attacks was to keep his well-armoured knights on the land flank, then, when the attacking Turks and their small horses were flagging, he would deploy his bowmen through the ranks of mounted spearmen, causing very high casualties among the closely grouped Turks at short range. In this way, Richard's crusaders advanced southwards beyond Haifa and Caesarea – slowly because Richard was not prepared to outrun his shipping support, and the wind was not favourable: also in the Mediterranean heat he was not prepared to demand too much of his knights and serjeants,[2] particularly those who were heavily armoured. There had already been heavy casualties from the effects of the heat.

Saladin chose to try to halt Richard's advance at Arsuf, just north of Jaffa, but, once again the tactic of spearmen and armour alternating with bowmen was too much for Saladin's 'light cavalry'. In spite of his frustration, the watching Saladin found himself admiring the way in which Richard was mounted at the head of his troops: indeed on one occasion when Richard's horse was down, Saladin actually despatched a groom to him with two fresh horses.

---

[2] In modern parlance, the rank and file.

In spite of being outnumbered initially[3] the English tactics had worn down Saladin's Turks and Arabs, and in the day's battle at Arsuf the final cavalry charge being led by Richard sealed the first real victory over Saladin in open battle since the humiliating defeat of the Christians at Hattin in 1187. This success greatly boosted Richard's already high reputation, while Saladin's standing after the Arsuf battle on 7th September 1191 had been severely damaged. He withdrew his forces south-east to Ramleh to cover the approaches to Jerusalem.

In fact neither of the great commanders was anxious to resume the conflict. Richard, who had never succeeded in shaking off his fever, was exhausted and ill, and Saladin, although reinforced since Arsuf, was more interested in ensuring the soundness of the Jerusalem defences than challenging Richard to another major battle.

With the Saracens concentrated on the routes to Jerusalem, the Frankish forces moved along the coast to Jaffa. This threatened Ascalon which was the gateway for reinforcements for Saladin from Egypt, so he set about its destruction in a 'scorched earth' policy designed to make it a less attractive target for his enemies – a tactic that had failed to work at Jaffa and was unsuccessful, too, at Ascalon. In the event Richard's men captured both and rebuilt them.

Having spent several weeks at Jaffa and Ascalon, with only the occasional Turkish raid to disturb them, the crusaders and

---

[3] It is doubtful if Richard's crusaders ever numbered more than 8,000 all told.

their allies the Frankish Templars and Hospitallers, seeing that Saladin was dismantling outposts rather than strengthening them, turned their attention to their real goal, Jerusalem.

Richard was always ready to use diplomacy either in concert with, or in place of, military force and from early October onwards he was probing, through Saladin's brother, al-Adil, the possibility of a negotiated truce. One proposal was for al-Adil to rule over Palestine and marry Richard's sister, Queen Joan of Sicily, and for the latter to control the coastal strip conquered by Richard. The ruling pair would live in Jerusalem which would be accessible to Christians; and the True Cross should be returned to them. Finally, the resident Knights Templar and Knights Hospitaller should have their possessions in Palestine returned to them.

Nothing came of this proposal, nor of some variations put forward on the one hand by Richard through Humphrey of Toron or on the other by Conrad trying to make his own bargain with Saladin. Between the Saracens and the Franks some fitful raiding and spasmodic attacks took place while these proposals and counter-proposals were kept in play, and King Richard maintained his customary careless impetuosity by twice putting himself at risk of capture but, with the onset of the winter rains, Saladin and his army settled for winter quarters in Jerusalem.

Richard and his men, now reinforced from Acre, moved unopposed to the ruins of Ramleh and, having spent November and some of December there without much interference, took the opportunity provided by Saladin's retirement to Jerusalem to follow up as far as Latrun, some twenty-five kilometres from the

Holy City, where they spent Christmas. After Christmas the weather deteriorated still further, but the proximity of Jerusalem remained a magnet for most of those who, after all, had already sacrificed much to reach it. So, enthusiastic in spite of the conditions, the crusaders continued up into the hills only some fifteen kilometres from the city.

Without firm local advice and intelligence from the Knights Templar and Hospitaller for whom Palestine was, after all, their chosen home country, it is probable that the strong Christian desire once again to rule Jerusalem would have driven Richard and his crusaders to assault the city even in the storms and mud that lay ahead. Once in Jerusalem, though, and in the face of the heavy losses involved in the assault, Richard's army would immediately have been threatened by an encircling Arab force from Egypt. It would have been completely cut off from the supporting crusader fleet and was already suffering from lack of supplies and from disease. In any event, the crusaders, even if they succeeded in capturing Jerusalem, would not have remained there. Their task done, they would have returned home and the local Franks would not have had the strength to retain either Jerusalem or, indeed, much of the coastal area captured by Richard.

The idea of retreating, leaving a military task uncompleted, was never likely to appeal to Richard but the clear strategic sense of the Frankish knights' argument was undeniable. What is more, information from Normandy and England pointed more and more clearly to the way in which his brother John was using his absence to usurp his authority and to attempt to detach some of his barons and vassals from him. Furthermore, Richard's allies were beginning to drift away. The French were already beginning to retreat piecemeal to Jaffa. After a council meeting at Ramleh, Richard ordered a retreat to Ascalon where the army spent the next three months making it a strong fortified town again.

The next diversion was a fight for the base at Acre between the crusaders from Pisa, purporting to be fighting for King Guy, and those from Genoa, professing to be fighting on behalf of the French, in the persons of Hugh of Burgundy and Conrad. Richard had to return to Acre to bang heads together and safeguard the port. It was clear that if there was to be any long-term gain from this the Third Crusade, all the quarrelling between those claiming to be on the same side had to be stopped. One of the sources of this perpetual internal strife was the unresolved problem of who was to rule the Franks in Palestine – Guy, the nominal King of Jerusalem, or Conrad, the actual ruler of Tyre. Richard called a council of all the knights and barons in Palestine and put it to the vote: this was overwhelmingly for Conrad. It was planned that he would be crowned at Acre but before this could happen Conrad was ambushed and murdered by two of the Assassin[4] sect, apparently because Conrad had caused offence to Sinan the Assassin leader.

---

[4] An extreme Muslim faction formed at the end of the 11th century as a result of disagreement with the Ismaili branch of their faith, originally over the caliphate succession. The only way in which members of the sect dealt with opposition, whether from other Muslims or non-Muslims, was by murder: hence came the verb to 'assassinate'.

The places of both King Guy and Marquis Conrad were filled, with goodwill on all sides, by Henry II of Champagne, the nephew of both Richard and Philip Augustus. Henry had already established himself as a gentle nobleman and a competent military commander. He had commanded the besieging forces at Acre from July 1190, taking over from King Guy, and had remained in charge until Richard's arrival. Since that time he had loyally represented Richard in many delicate negotiations. The appointment of Henry as the new King of Jerusalem (or at least of the coastal conquests) was further endorsed and happily completed by his early marriage to Conrad's widow which came to be a most successful and happy solution.

In this summer of 1192, neither of the main protagonists in Palestine – Saladin and Richard – had the slightest wish to re-engage in major battles. Both were sick men and sick of battles which were generally promoted by others. The Frankish forces permanently stationed in Palestine, flushed with the settlement of the Guy–Conrad squabbles, were all for Richard leading a new assault on Jerusalem. Richard on the other hand, receiving news of Philip of France using his return from the Crusade to whittle away at Richard's possessions in Normandy, and of a dangerous alliance Philip had established with John to seize authority in England, was longing to end the Crusade and return home. The Turks chose this moment to attack Jaffa and Richard was once again involved in teaching tactical lessons to both sides. In spite of French pressure to exploit this defeat of Saladin's men by attacking Jerusalem (the motives of which Richard, probably rightly, distrusted) the mutual desire of Saladin and Richard and the Franks under Henry of Champagne for the fighting to end was bound to triumph. The peace treaty which brought the Third Crusade to an end was signed on 2nd September 1192. The Palestine coast remained Christian from Tyre down to Jaffa, but not as far as Ascalon: this area was to be ruled by Henry of Champagne as a Muslim protectorate. Muslims and Christians were to be able to have free passage through each other's territory, and Jerusalem would be open to pilgrims. On 29th September Richard saw his Queen, Berengaria, and Queen Joan sail for France from Acre. He and most of his crusaders followed on 9th October.

CHAPTER 7

'What we Chiefly Need'

King Richard I was certainly not to be one of England's 'sailor kings', though even one of those might have had second thoughts about embarking in a 12th-century galley at times of equinoctial gales. The vessel was a small one, chosen by Richard for speed rather than comfort and, because of this, his household and escort together amounted to only a score of people.

Richard's unhappy sea-going experiences continued. Storms forced his galley to take shelter at Corfu. With his small party Richard felt vulnerable to any but a very friendly ruler, and Emperor Isaac Angelus of Corfu was not such a one. Richard was now determined to keep his sea crossings to the minimum and, finding a buccaneering coastal vessel about to leave for the head of the Adriatic, he took passage with his small party.

Bad weather continued to dog King Richard, as did his misfortune. The galley was wrecked in the gulf on the coast of

1. St Edmund's Abbey before the Reformation. From a drawing by W.K. Hardy.

2. Master Hugo created carved bronze doors for the Abbey. The 12th century doors illustrated are at Benevento Cathedral in Campania and provide an idea of the task involved.

3. Framlingham Castle. The stronghold of the Bigod family and a headquarters for rebels against Henry II in the 12th century. An 18th century view of the castle engraved by Samuel and Nathaniel Buck.

4. The only whole 12th century relic of St Edmund's Abbey. This tower, the south gate leading to the west front of the Abbey, was built in the 1120s as part of Abbot Anselm's St James' Church for which it provided the bell tower. It still performs this function for what is now St Edmundsbury Cathedral, also dedicated to St James.

5. Part of the frontispiece for Jeremiah in the 'Bury Bible' one of the magnificent illustrations in Master Hugo's masterpiece. This illustrates the similarities between the attacking soldiers and those sleeping in the Easter scene from the cross below.

6. The Easter plaque on the 'Bury Cross'; showing the Angel and the three Marys at the tomb and the sleeping soldier guards.

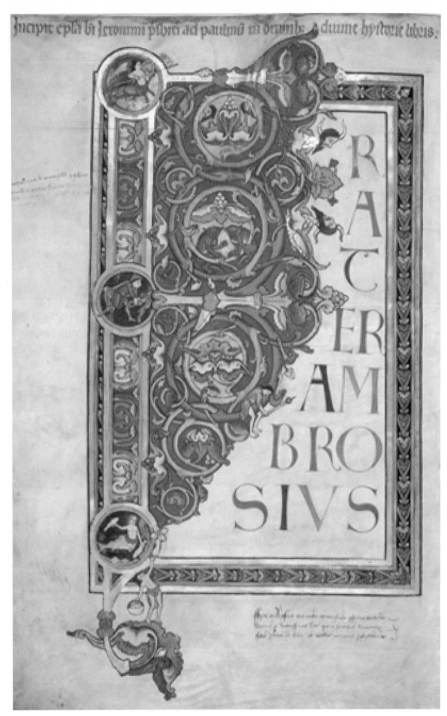

7. The opening page of the 'Bury Bible' which illustrates the scope of Master Hugo's talent.

8. The front of the 'Bury Cross' which, with illustrations 2, 5, 6 and 7, show the amazing extent of Master Hugo's creative skill.

9. Acre (or Akko). The walls of the old town on the open sea side. The only beach approach to the town was beyond the promontory to the north and the crusaders held this and used it for reinforcement and re-supply.

10. The surrender of Acre to King Richard (left) and King Philip Augustus of France (right) on 12th/13th July 1191. From a painting by Merry Joseph Blondel.

11. Richard I, from his effigy on his monument in the Abbey at Fontevrault where he is buried with his parents Henry II and Queen Eleanor. From an engraving by George Vertue.

12. Durrenstein (or Dürnstein) Castle on the River Danube, where King Richard was imprisoned by Leopold of Austria in 1193. From a drawing by H. Gransire.

13. The Bakony lowlands in Hungary today.

14. A remnant of the 12th century Cistercian Abbey at Zirc. The statue of St Imre on the top of the clustered column was placed there in 1751. The other remains of the medieval abbey were demolished during the eighteenth century when the present abbey was built. It was subsequently extended in both the 19th and 20th centuries.

the then province of Carniola.[1] Richard's party all survived, together with their minimal baggage which included the ivory cross in the care of Richard's one-time chaplain, William of Poitou, and Richard had the additional compensation that he was approaching friendly country. The Dalmatian coast bordered on the land of King Béla III of Hungary and his allies, the safe end of the old land route to the crusades, last used by Frederick 'Barbarossa'. However, the English party had some of Carinthia, Bavaria and Austria ahead of them if they were to start on the most direct route to the north-west, and in that direction Richard had few friends to help him on his way. The way home led initially through Austria and Bavaria which, in terms of rulers, meant the lands of Leopold and his sovereign, the German Emperor, Henry VI.

Leopold had neither forgotten nor forgiven the cavalier fashion in which Richard had had his Austrian banner thrown down at Acre when its owner had presumed to raise it alongside those who had actually brought about the crusade victory there; and Henry VI was an enemy of long standing. Apart from Béla III of Hungary, only Henry the Lion, Duke of Saxony, was a certain ally and he no longer held sway in Bavaria.

From the start of his journey King Richard had been prepared to make the journey incognito and as long as he was part of a group of just under twenty, the guise of pilgrims was just sustainable, provided that their possessions were commensurate

---

[1] Modern Trieste lies to the north-west of this.

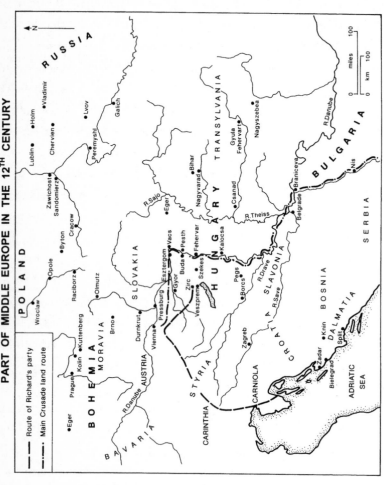

PART OF MIDDLE EUROPE IN THE 12TH CENTURY

and their attitudes, particularly to one another, consistent with their adopted role.

The news of Richard's shipping disasters was certainly known to those on the watch for him, and the size of his party, although some protection against footpads, was bound to be worthy of investigation and would not be sufficient defence against the sort of armed body Richard's enemies could deploy.

It was early days in their 'pilgrimage' when eight of the King's escort were captured in the mountainous area of Carinthia by one Meinhard of Görz, and the rest of the party had made only a little ground further north to Friesach when six more were captured the following night. The King, his chaplain and two others, William of Poitou and Thomas of Nontron, managed to get away into the darkness. Moving mostly at night and depending on snatched scraps of food from isolated habitations, this small group followed the valleys of the Rivers Mur and Mürz north-eastwards for another three days. Eventually the need for food overcame caution and Richard set off with his chaplain Anselm to buy food. They were captured just south of Vienna about ten days before Christmas. This was the quarry; the hunt was called off and the two survivors of the King's household made their escape.

So it was that Duke Leopold and Meinhard arrived at Ratisbon on 6th January 1193 with the King of England as their prisoner – and the bargaining began. Although Henry VI, Emperor of the

Holy Roman Empire and King of Germany, was Leopold's sovereign, the latter was not about to hand his captor to Henry without exacting some reward. He would have been as aware as his master that King Henry was in dire need of help. Germany at that time was divided into many princedoms and about half of these were involved in quarrels amongst themselves and schemes to unseat the Emperor. The acquisition of the King of England as captive would present Henry with a card of very considerable political importance, as well as a probable source of wealth to his treasury.

Leopold had his price, and until this had been accepted by Henry, Richard was his prisoner. Indeed, once Henry was convinced that Richard was safely in custody, Leopold returned him to imprisonment in the castle at Dürnstein[2] in Austria out of reach of any possible kidnapping attempt: mutual trust between rulers was a rare commodity in the 12th century.

The bargaining continued into mid-February, ending with a true King's ransom of 100,000 marks as the price for King Richard's release. Of this, 75,000 marks would come to Leopold, 50,000 of which would be disguised as a dowry for Richard's niece, Eleanor of Brittany, who was betrothed to one of Leopold's sons. In addition, Richard would have to contract to provide 50 galleys, 200 knights and 100 crossbowmen to help Henry's next invasion of Sicily.

On the basis of this agreement, Richard was released from

---

[2] Also known as Durrenstein.

Dürnstein Castle on the Danube into Henry's hands, though only after Leopold had received 200 hostages from the German Emperor as surety for the latter's fulfilment of the contract.

Of the many who had heard the news of Richard's capture with rejoicing, the principals were Philip Augustus of France and Richard's brother John, who had been partners for some years in respectively trying to take over Richard, Duke of Aquitaine's lands on the Continent and usurp the throne of England. Philip lost no time in moving into Normandy, seized Gisors and was threatening Rouen, then being defended by Robert, Earl of Leicester.[3] John, in the early days of Richard's imprisonment, spread the word that his brother was dead, then that he might not be but would never return, thereby acquiring some of Richard's weaker supporters. He tried to secure King William of Scotland as an ally in stirring up a rebellion in England, but Richard had been generous to William in the past and the latter remained loyal.

The most vulnerable time for Richard's throne was while there was only rumour, which his enemies could manipulate. Once firm information was available his friends could take positive steps. The first to learn what had happened appears to have been Richard's right-hand man on the Third Crusade, Hubert Walter, Bishop of Salisbury. He had set out from Outremer for Sicily at a different time from Richard, had heard there of his capture and had made the best time possible directly to Germany to find him.

---

[3] The 4th Earl, son of the rebel and later to support Richard's successor John.

Richard was confined by Henry VI at Speyer on the Rhine, having been moved gradually westward since leaving Austria. Bishop Hubert Walter had succeeded in finding him at Ochsenfurt on the River Main further east where Leopold had halted for a time in February, and it was from there that the Bishop made the best time he could to give England, notably Richard's mother Queen Eleanor and the justiciars, together the Regency Council, the facts about their king.

On his arrival in England, Hubert Walter convened a meeting of the Regency Council to review the situation. The council realised that Richard must be as ignorant of the situation in England as they had been of his circumstances, and two Cistercian monks, the Abbots of Buxley and Robertsbridge were sent to Germany to give him the full picture and, in turn, to establish what needed to be done to achieve his return. Hubert Walter made a return visit, and saw King Richard finally installed by Henry VI at Speyer before returning to England with the monks on 20th April, bearing letters from Richard to Queen Eleanor and the council. Among the matters covered in them were the need to raise the very large sum of 100,000 marks (of which 70,000 would have to be paid before Henry VI would release Richard), and the King's wish that Bishop Hubert Walter should become Archbishop of Canterbury in the vacancy caused by the death of Reginald de Bohun, who had died after a very brief tenure.

At Speyer that Easter of 1193 Henry VI put Richard on trial. The charges were:

- betraying the Holy Land
- plotting the murder of Conrad of Montferrat
- breaking previous agreements with Henry VI

King Richard's period of captivity had so far brought out the very best in him. He showed little or no bitterness that after an exhausting series of battles in which, on most occasions, success had been as a result of his own personal courage and leadership, after some perilous sea voyages and, finally, considerable hardship in his overland journey, he was the captive of a much lesser man whom he must have despised. Throughout his imprisonment he had conducted himself with dignity and had shown quiet confidence that all would eventually be well in spite of all the machinations of Philip Augustus, the treachery of his brother John, and the disloyalty of some of his knights and vassals both in England and on the Continent. But it was in front of Henry's court that Richard showed why, for all his faults, he had always stood out as a lion among jackals. His response to Henry's somewhat trumped-up charges was so forceful and convincingly dismissive that it was soon clear that the court was won over. Sensing this, Henry VI, who had fewer political prizes to gain than Philip of France or John 'Lackland', instead of pressing the charges publicly made his peace with Richard and vowed to help to reconcile him with Philip.

For all these gestures of peace, Henry was not prepared to lose the fortune which he and Leopold were planning to extract from England: only now this was to be more in the nature of fees and expenses for the trouble to which the captors had been put. It would be a long time before this considerable sum could be raised, and in the meanwhile Richard, although first confined to a castle at Trifels, near Speyer, was allowed to rejoin Henry's imperial household at Hagenau and to maintain something of a small court of his own. This enabled him to work constructively, through letters and messengers, towards both the running of his kingdom and the raising of his ransom which, for all the euphemisms used, is precisely what it was. He also showed his innate political sense in establishing a degree of good relations with both Henry VI and some of the princes, both lay and ecclesiastical, who were Henry's vassals, with a view to having them on his side in the future. This was a policy by no means unwelcome to Henry, whose main concern was to ensure that Philip of France's expansionist ideas were kept in check. While he was so engaged there was much complementary action in train in England.

CHAPTER 8

'To Give a Hand'

The capture of King Richard was eventually to have reverberations throughout Europe, but one of the earliest reactions was that of his brother John. He had hurried to Philip Augustus of France to make plans to acquire as many as possible of Richard's lands while he was safely neutralised in Austria or Germany. To assist in cementing this Anglo-French alliance, which was his lifeline, John contracted to marry Philip's daughter, Alice.

Surprisingly, because he had already gained considerable experience of his mother's grip on affairs of state, John seemed to be reckoning without her influence. Eleanor and the Chancellor, William Longchamp, were just as quickly into action as her son and rapidly exacted renewed oaths of allegiance to Richard from those of his subjects whom John was likely to try to suborn. They also reviewed the state of readiness of the key castles and set in train the necessary measures to prepare for possible assaults.

The first direct news of Richard came in February 1193 when Bishop Hubert Walter returned to England from seeing Richard at Ochsenfurt and addressed a Regency Council meeting. He was able to reassure them about Richard's health and the latter's attitude of mind, which was one of calm optimism; also his immediate destination. The council approved the measures that had already been taken to guard against further erosion by John, and to consider future possibilities. The members also examined ways of meeting the demand for ransom, which was already being talked of as 100,000 marks, and deputed William Longchamp (already on the Continent) to open negotiations and act as mediator with Henry VI with whom he was on good terms.

Meanwhile, to fill in some detail and provide Richard with a permanent line of communication, two Cistercian monks were sent to him, monks being thought more acceptable to Henry than envoys of a more political or military nature.

John had not been idle and had strengthened his garrisons at Windsor and Wallingford castles which he had secured even before Richard had left for the crusade. At the time that Richard was about to have to defend himself orally against Henry's charges at Speyer, John was having to defend himself militarily at Windsor against attacks by Walter of Coutance, Bishop of Lincoln, while his garrison at Tickhill was equally under siege from Hugh de Puiset, Bishop of Durham.

The impact of all the events in the Mediterranean area from 1191 onwards on the Abbey at Bury St Edmunds, and on Abbot Samson in particular, was strong and lasting. The close ties of the Abbey with the King ensured that particularly strenuous efforts were made at St Edmundsbury to help in raising funds for the cost of the crusade, and these inevitably had to be extended by the long period of the secondary battles involved in Sicily and Cyprus (although after Cyprus Richard's crusaders could justifiably have been regarded as self-supporting at the very least).

On Samson himself, though, the repercussions were very personal. Apart from his clear admiration for and affinity with King Richard, there is no doubt that the crusades, indeed the whole struggle between the Angevin House and Philip of France, between Richard and John, was one which Samson experienced vicariously; and it must have been very frustrating. He had, after all, genuinely greatly wished to be with Richard as a crusader himself.

At the meeting of barons in 1192 when the capture of Richard became known, it was Samson who leapt to his feet and volunteered to search for Richard, in disguise if necessary. It would have added to his frustration that Richard's whereabouts and situation in fact became public so soon. He also cannot fail to have been keenly disappointed to discover on his visit to King Richard at Speyer that he no longer had the ivory cross and had not seen it since his capture.

When Philip Augustus and John went into action against Richard to take advantage of his imprisonment, there was no holding back the militant Abbot. Having first exercised his clerical role to excommunicate all those talking arms against Richard's supporters, he then took arms himself against John in joining the besieging force under Walter of Coutance at Windsor.

In a way it must have added to his frustration that another

whom he had excommunicated in the past, William Longchamp, although banned from the shores of England and distrusted by Eleanor and her council, remained one of Richard's trusted friends and was to be instrumental in negotiating his eventual release. Indeed, it was while these negotiations were in train in April 1193 that, at Bishop Hubert's instigation, a truce was arranged with John at Windsor. Little as Samson would have been prepared to admit it, this was probably for the best from his point of view since, as his chronicler Jocelin put it, 'he gained more fame for his advice than for his chivalry'. It was also a great additional expense for the Abbey maintaining an armoured Abbot and a large number of knights in a siege at Windsor.

The truce at Windsor was mirrored in the wider theatre by the news of the alliance of Henry VI and Richard; an alliance directed more to the disadvantage of the King of France than to the advantage of the King of England, and which was accompanied by the news, brought back by William Longchamp, that the price for Richard's return had increased to 150,000 marks. This was now disguised partly as the extra costs of Richard's captivity, latterly including a small court at Hagenau, and the price of releasing Richard from the alternative 'tribute' of assisting Henry in an attack on Sicily.

The imminent release of King Richard had been signalled to John by Philip in the terms, 'Look to yourself. The Devil is loosed' which had John hurrying to Paris and quickly handing over to Philip some of his recent gains in Normandy and Touraine. With Richard's subjects now at their wits' end to raise an enormous sum of money from lands already heavily burdened with the costs of war, and with Henry's empire linked with Richard's ability, all sides were, for a time, seeking an armistice.

Philip was only too happy to sign a treaty with Richard's envoys which left the French holding on to some of their recent gains, not to mention John's recent peace-offering.

Many suggestions had been received, both from Richard and William Longchamp, for raising the ransom money, and Eleanor and the Regency Council had had to steel themselves to really vigorous measures. A tax of twenty-five per cent was called for from each person (including some clergy who had hitherto been exempt), knights had each to find twenty shillings, churches were to provide all their valuables (Richard himself, had demanded this) and Cistercian establishments, which could not have valuables, had to provide a year's output of wool from their sheep. All the treasures collected in England had to be taken to St Paul's in London where they were kept under the seals of Queen Eleanor and Walter of Coutance, being supervised by Bishop Hubert Walter, Bishop Richard Fitz Neal, William, Earl of Arundel, Hamelin, Earl Warenne (King Richard's uncle) and the Mayor of London. Richard's possessions on the continent were not absolved from contributing and collections continued to take place through 1194.

At St Edmundsbury Abbey Samson, while ensuring that no church or churchman failed to meet their obligations, gave encouragement to those clergy who were prepared to save their church plate by providing the equivalent in money from their own pockets to do so. For all his admiration and loyalty for King Richard, Samson was quite adamant that he would never permit St Edmund's shrine to be stripped of any of its precious metal to contribute to the King's ransom – 'nor is there any man who would get me to agree to it'.

When King Richard and his chaplain, Anselm, failed to return from their foraging near Vienna, William of Poitou and Thomas of Nontron feared the worst but, other than taking even greater precautions to keep under cover, could do little initially until they could discover what had happened. After thirty-six hours had passed with no signs of the King and Anselm, and with nothing to eat, William ventured to the outskirts of a village, leaving Thomas with their packs. As they had done until now he continued to pose as a pilgrim, offering to pay for food with silver or small items of jewellery which they had left, though more often than not, no payment was asked from 'pilgrims'.

Having acquired sufficient food for at least for two days on very tight rations, William and Thomas determined to leave the confines of Leopold's territory and Henry's empire as soon as possible. Through talks with other crusaders in Outremer they knew of the old crusader routes through King Béla's friendly kingdom of Hungary; one of these followed the Danube Valley through Vienna to Belgrade but another well-established route entered Hungary from Austria at Sopron and went south-eastwards to pick up the Danube Valley further south in Hungary; and

Sopron and the Hungarian border were only some twenty miles to the south-east.

The going was very rough and there were times when it was very tempting to discard all but the very minimum essential baggage but William, an ordained monk, in particular was adamant that the ivory cross was not only in trust from Richard but was a link with St Edmund which they would sever at their peril. Also, during the crusade the ability to separate the upper and lower shafts so that the cross could be carried as three lengths of ivory not more than three inches wide and wrapped in cloth within a small valise made it easily portable. The existence of the cross not only gave them, or at least William, a feeling of being protected, but also would provide evidence as to their role as pilgrims if circumstances called for this.

As long as they remained in potentially hostile territory the pair were fearful that even apparently friendly villagers could give them away, and the lack of firm information about the rest of Richard's party made contact with habitation, while desirable from the point of view of hearing news, equally dangerous should the local population be on watch for them. Their hopes and prayers were that they might find a monastery where, irrespective of the order it might embrace, they could expect to find help and protection. As crusaders they were confident that the Pope would shield them against enemies of those who had 'taken the cross' (they would have taken great heart if they had known that the Pope was to excommunicate Leopold for imprisoning Richard). They did not know of any monastery nearby, but the Benedictines had long been in Hungary and they were aware that the Cistercians were now also well established; in addition, they might providentially encounter an itinerant monk.

They had good grounds for expecting help from Cistercians. The Third Crusade had been preached, and in many ways sponsored, by the Cistercians. A notable English Cistercian, Baldwin of Ford, became Archbishop of Canterbury and accompanied Richard on the crusade, only to die at Acre; and the Knights Templar who were virtually the Cistercians' fighting arm, were well established in Hungary (indeed a detachment of the Templars, who had fought under Richard in Palestine, had been part of his escort and been captured in Austria).

William and Thomas did not spare themselves. For the next three days they drove themselves across the high ground of Burgenland towards the great lake of Neusiedler See (Fertö) just across the Austro-Hungarian border. It was desperately rough going at times, avoiding all well-worn tracks but they managed to cover an average of ten miles a day and were rewarded on the third day by the sight of a village in stark contrast to those they had seen in Austria. The homes were low, in some instances the eaves of the thatched roofs almost reaching the ground because the floors were generally below ground level, and there was a primitive look to the whole village. William was sufficiently confident that this was no Austrian habitation to approach one of the villagers, and an attempt to converse was all that was needed. They were in King Béla's country.

CHAPTER 9

'Walk With Us'

The political manoeuvring between Henry VI, Philip Augustus, John and some of their vassals concerning the captivity of King Richard became even more feverish as the time approached when the major part of his ransom would be available. Concessions made to John by Richard, who never took his brother's efforts at subversion seriously, were frustrated by the total rejection of John by the majority of Richard's subjects. John, for his part, continued to try to buy Philip's support by passing over to him lands which were Angevin by any calculation and were essential parts of Angevin defences.

As part of the numerous and increasing conditions for his release, Richard had had to pay homage to Henry as Holy Roman Emperor, and to receive England and his possessions on the mainland as a king, within that empire. However, he was granted some new lands in Europe in addition: not because of Henry's newly discovered admiration or affection for Richard but rather to bolster the German Emperor's campaign against Philip. At the same time Richard contracted to pay Henry the equivalent of £5,000 annually, adding yet more to the onerous financial burden already bearing heavily on his people (and particularly his ecclesiastical establishments) stemming from the Third Crusade.

Philip, meanwhile, was endeavouring to form an alliance with Denmark by marrying into Cnut's family which gave him some sort of very tenuous claim to the English throne; or might have done if he had not rejected his wife immediately after the marriage. Finding so many of their schemes in the end unprofitable, and seeing the time of Richard's release fast approaching, Philip and John made one last attempt to bribe Henry to keep Richard in captivity; bidding varied from £1,000 a month to a lump sum of 80,000 marks to keep him to the end of the military campaigning season (late autumn) or 150,000 marks for a year or to make Richard their prisoner. This approach succeeded in postponing Richard's release, which had been due on 17th January 1194, and Henry called a meeting at Mainz of all the princes of his empire for 2nd February to make known these new offers: with some effrontery he also invited Queen Eleanor, Walter of Coutance and William Longchamp who were already in Germany, having arrived with a rather impressive entourage on the expectation of greeting a free Richard and escorting him back to England.

Naturally, there was considerable anger among the English party, bearing in mind the large amounts of money and valuables that had already been handed over and the length of time that Richard had already spent in captivity. Fortunately, a high proportion of the German princes, who had no love for the Philip and John coalition, shared the English repugnance for this development and, in any event, were keen to begin to receive their share of the ransom already paid (especially Leopold of Austria, who was present) with the result that on 4th February 1194 King Richard was brought to Queen Eleanor as a free man by the Archbishop of Mainz and Cologne.

King Richard maintained throughout his life an extraordinary capacity to do things in his own time, apparently disregarding the pressures from others or even of events. He must have been aware of the feverish activity of his enemies to take the most advantage of his time still in captivity, and to make as much ground as possible before his release, and yet he made an almost leisurely progress from Speyer back to England. He visited Cologne and spent three days there with the Archbishop. He and his party then stayed with the River Rhine and it was a fortnight later before he was in Louvain. Eventually he reached Brussels three weeks after departure from Henry's Court. At Antwerp ships were waiting to take him home, yet he still took time to spend five days visiting the Netherlands coast before at last setting sail for England. For all that this might have the appearance of fiddling while Rome was burning, though, there may well have been many lasting benefits from this apparently casual behaviour. Many allies from the German states, particularly the lower Rhineland and the low countries, later emerged. Also many potential supporters of Philip in the coastal areas of the Netherlands and Flanders might have felt uncomfortable at the King of England and his fleet in the waters near them. Some will have recalled a similar slow approach to the Holy Land which left defeated rulers of Sicily and Cyprus in its wake.

In any event this regal disregard of the machinations of smaller mortals was so much a part of Richard and so much in line with his attitude on the battlefield that it further added to his reputation and prestige as a leader, and presented to those who were potential allies or enemies an inviting contrast to the vacillating and fickle John.

King Richard landed at Sandwich on 13th March 1194, the best part of four years after he had left for the crusade, and with his return the threat of a strong John and Philip of France coalition faded. Philip lost no time in setting out to secure the land on the Continent which John had ceded to him in the hope of thus gaining French support against his brother. At the same time in England John's castles at Lancaster, Marlborough, Nottingham, St Michael's Mount and Tickhill had already surrendered to forces loyal to Queen Eleanor, Richard and his Chancellor, and were mostly under episcopal leadership. Prince John was virtually 'Lackland' again.

The return of King Richard was a cause of much rejoicing in England, even though the nation had hardly seen anything of him and had been drained of both money and treasures since his coronation to pay for his adventures abroad, his release from captivity and to quell John's rebellion. Richard's first call was to the Abbey at Canterbury to give thanks at the shrine of St Thomas for his safe return.

Richard was met near Rochester on 14th March by Hubert

Walter, the recently appointed Archbishop of Canterbury his great supporter during the crusade and, latterly, virtual regent in England, who then became part of Richard's retinue bound for London. They reached the city on 16th March and it was a triumphal entry. Tales of Richard's courage and leadership in battle had been brought back by returning crusaders, London was decorated with flags and banners and the streets were full of cheering crowds, for whom there was at last a king with a reputation of which they found it easy to be proud and a ruler whom they could trust to restore stability and influence to the country.

The King went in procession to St Paul's Cathedral where he received the welcome of the clergy. While he was there he would almost certainly have received accounts of the collection of his ransom, as the Cathedral had been the centre to which all the contributions had been sent. After a day at Westminster, the King moved on. It is likely that London and its riches made a greater impact on some of the foreigners in Richard's retinue than on the King himself. He never gave the impression of being greatly attached to London (he had, after all, been on record as being 'prepared to sell London, if necessary' to raise funds for his campaigns).

Next, and undoubtedly to Abbot Samson's joy, Richard headed for Bury St Edmunds to give thanks at St Edmund's shrine. Strangely, the monk at the Abbey who painstakingly recorded most of Samson's abbacy in considerable detail, Brother Jocelin, remains silent about this event. However, it is certain that Richard would have had much to tell Samson and would have wished to express his gratitude to his loyal friends, even though Samson had rightly refused to surrender some of the riches from St Edmund's shrine as a contribution to the King's ransom.

The accompanying court included Queen Eleanor but almost certainly was without William Longchamp, who would not have been welcome at Bury St Edmunds: but a long celebratory stay was not in prospect. The priority now, both from the royal party's point of view and that of staunch supporter Samson, was a plan to deal with Prince John, and a meeting of the Great Council was scheduled at Nottingham on 30th March with this subject at the top of the agenda.

Nevertheless, Abbot Samson and his officials had much to show Richard of developments in the Abbey and Queen Eleanor had not visited Bury St Edmunds for many years. Much work had been done to the Abbey towers: the central western tower and that by St Katherine's Chapel finished and, inside St James' Church, work on the pulpit, choir and rood screens was complete. When Samson was showing his paintings and elegiac verse in the choir, their relationship with some of the carvings on Master Hugo's cross could not have failed to lead to talk of the loss of the latter and to Richard's account of its value to him during the crusade.

At the Great Council at Nottingham, reports on the military situation in England would have been very encouraging for the King's group. Prince John had no stronghold now and although he had been given by Philip Augustus theoretical custody over three castles in Normandy, he had no prospect of being able to hold them against Richard once the latter had assembled a force on the continent finally to settle his continuing feud with Philip.

On 17th April 1194 Richard had a second coronation, at Winchester, while up and down the country Hubert Walter was raising both funds and armies for Richard's impending battles against Philip to regain the possessions which the Frenchman and John had seized while he was on the crusade. On 12th May Richard sailed from Portsmouth and shortly afterwards Queen Eleanor managed to achieve a reconciliation between her sons, Richard and John, and herself.

For all that the situation was improving for Richard, there was no corresponding deterioration in the affairs of his great rival Henry VI, King of Germany and Holy Roman Emperor. Indeed Tancred, the King of Sicily, so humiliated by Richard on his way to Acre, had died. There was only a child to succeed him and it was an easy matter for Henry to add Sicily to his possessions. There would be no question of a free and friendly passage over any of Henry's land for William of Poitou and Thomas of Nontron and the Bury Cross in hiding just over the Hungarian border.

CHAPTER 10

'I Weep For You'

The country in which William and Thomas were hoping for a safe passage in 1192 was a flourishing monarchy. Under King Béla III, Hungary had expanded both to the south to envelop Dalmatia and the north to annex Galicia. It was, however, largely the monarchy itself which was flourishing; King Béla's revenue was about equal in value to that of Philip of France. His people, though, remained poor and, for the most part, led lives in somewhat primitive conditions.

In an effort to develop his country to more nearly approach the nations of western Europe, King Béla gave considerable encouragement to nationals from those countries to work and settle in Hungary. So the local inhabitants were well accustomed to a steady flow of Italians, Germans and Walloons (the latter also, for some reason, frequently referred to as 'Italians') moving towards centres of population, a fact which helped considerably to enable the two crusaders to pass virtually unnoticed.

Although there had been fears on Béla's accession that he

might embrace Greek Orthodoxy, he became a strongly Catholic monarch. Christianity had been well established in Hungary since the time of King Stephen.[1] There were eight bishoprics which, in their earliest days, had all been held by foreigners. The first order of monks in the country had been Benedictine and monasteries had been established from the late 10th century onwards, but in the 12th century the strongest order was Cistercian and, in particular, King Béla had richly endowed Cistercian monasteries at Igris, Pilis, Szentgotthárd and Zirc. All this was to prove helpful to the crusaders.

The Hungarian countryside was a mixture of wooded mountains and low-lying plains, the latter being well-watered and providing excellent pasture for the many domestic animals. The River Danube flows north to south through approximately the centre of Hungary and in the western half, where William and Thomas were slowly making their way, the main features were the forested Bakony mountains in the north-west and Lake Balaton to the south of these.

Recollection of stories told of the routes of the Second Crusade, and used by Emperor Frederick Barbarossa in the Third, would have drawn William and Thomas to take a direction almost due east towards Györ (roughly parallel to the valley of the Danube where it flows east to west along the Austro-Hungarian border – though they were almost certainly unaware of that). A more south-easterly route was inevitably forced upon them in

---

[1] Subsequently, like Edmund, to be Saint Stephen.

order to clear a large expanse of water[2] and as the ground became noticeably easier to the south this would have better suited the travellers – Thomas was in a weakened condition from the fever which had affected so many during the Third Crusade, including, at times, King Richard himself.

The old crusade land route had the attractions that those living along it had a reputation for helping crusaders, and that it was on land bordering this route that the Knights Templar had established their forts. The first day's travelling by the refugees must have been one of considerable caution. They could not regard themselves as being free from pursuit by Austrians over a very open border, and until they had established themselves under the protection of someone of authority in Hungary they would have felt very vulnerable.

The countryside eastward became flatter and more watery. It was sparsely populated and the people were small in stature and roughly dressed in thick woollen clothing. Wherever there were small settlements there were glimpses of a few sheep, goats and occasionally cattle, grazing the good green pasture that abounded.

After a day's travel there appeared the outskirts of a fairly large collection of dwellings on a small river, where there seemed to be a number of people with more of the look of western Europeans. Nevertheless, no refugee from Austria could feel sufficiently far from the border to risk any open approach. However, it seemed wise to keep near the river, since it clearly

---

[2] The Neusiedler See.

meant proximity to settlements and future supplies, and it continued to lead them eastwards away from the border area and towards the main artery which would have been used by crusaders. One of the advantages of this relative 'highway' was that it was likely to be policed by the Templars who, as Cistercians, would probably be able to help with both protection and guidance to monasteries.

The fever was progressively weakening Thomas. It became necessary either to find shelter and rest soon or to acquire some form of transport to carry him. Certainly, without the latter the chances of the pair being able to cover more than six miles a day were slim. So it must have been with great relief that early in the day, by a river (evidently called the Rába), they encountered a group of Templars riding from Szombathely near the Austrian border, towards Györ to the north-east. After hearing the crusaders' story, the Templars willingly provided them with some generous rations and a pack horse to carry Thomas. They also suggested a route eastwards towards one Benedictine and two Cistercian monasteries which would avoid the worst of the very steep and heavily forested country of the Bakony mountains.

With this new help and encouraged by the, at best, friendliness and, at worst, indifference of the very mixed races which they encountered, the two crusaders moved on at a much better pace, still keeping to the flat watery places which made progress easier.

Communication with the people they encountered was not difficult. The number of westerners of various origins that had emigrated to Hungary in recent years meant that French or Latin was understood by a surprising number of inhabitants: help with maintaining direction was not too difficult in consequence.

After a further two days, however, it was clear that Thomas would need proper medical care if he was to survive. At a place called Pápa, William found a hospice where the monks offered to care for Thomas and, if his condition improved sufficiently, to try to get him home by sea from Dalmatia. They also promised that, if their resources proved inadequate to effect a cure, they would transfer him to a big hospital at Esztergom in the north.

William, himself feeling weak and weary, must have been glad to accept the monks' offer that he should stay with them for a few days. However, on the second day of his stay a monk arrived from Szombathely who was on his way back to the Cistercian monastery at Zirc. He was its sacrist and was well informed about the supply routes in and out of Hungary. He was confident that he could arrange a safe passage home for William: he was also enthralled by the ivory cross. William was as stout-hearted as any of Richard's crusaders, but it had been a harassing and physically demanding journey at the end of a long campaign, and the prospect of many hundreds of miles ahead of him without escort, or even companions, before reaching home had filled him with foreboding. The Cistercian offer must have appeared as literally a godsend.

They set off the next day, well provisioned and well mounted, and headed north-east, first across the lowlands and then the northern lower slopes of the Bakony mountains. The Cistercian sacrist, whose name was Alban, was both a reliable guide and a good companion, and William and he found little difficulty in conversing, mostly in Latin. The Hungarian was of Italian origin and as William had spent some time in Rome there was much common ground – and Benedictine William had no theological difficulties with Cistercians.

After two days' journey, and as the countryside became more afforested and the ground rougher on the lower slopes of the Bakony mountains, it became apparent that William, too, had not escaped the infection which had gripped Thomas. The disease had been widespread among the crusaders and as it took different forms it was almost certainly a variety of malaria which, at that time, was very prevalent in parts of the Middle East. On some days William seemed to have recovered but when the fever returned it seemed even more debilitating. It was therefore with considerable relief that the companions came in sight of some large buildings and Alban announced their arrival at Zirc.

During their long journey William had heard from Alban a clear description of the life in a Cistercian monastery: the emphasis on simplicity and a rigid interpretation of the original Benedictine rule (with which in a much diluted form William was, to some extent, familiar): the reliance on work on the land for sustenance and the use of lay brothers to provide enough labour force for this. Although in later years the flourishing of Cistercian establishments through acquisition of more and more land actually worked against the Cistercian ideal of frugality, at this time in Hungary Alban warned William to expect an institution devoid of elaborate decoration, valuables or colourful artefacts. By this time the only valuable or artefact that William had in his baggage and accoutrements was Hugo's cross. Any Cistercian cross would be wooden and, at its most decorative, only painted,[3] but Alban assured William that the walrus cross would be accepted at the monastery as a personal possession for the period of time that William had to stay to recover before moving on; he would, though, need to keep it by him and let it be regarded as his personal property.

William received a warm welcome at Zirc. As a crusader he was bound to have been well received but, as an ex-chaplain to King Richard he possessed additional prestige, since Richard had been known to donate a church to Cistercians in England and was step-brother of Marguerite, King Béla III's wife – and Hungary's King was a staunch supporter of the Cistercians. William was housed in the lay brothers' infirmary (where he kept the ivory cross in his valise) and was given every care. However, he could not conceal his anxiety to return to England as soon as possible, and Alban set about the task of planning a secure and comfortable passage for him down to Dalmatia and then by sea in easy stages to France. Awareness that this was all in train encouraged William towards quick recovery, but in the end it was not to be. A week after his arrival at Zirc, William had a violent recurrence of fever and his weakened state meant that all the efforts of the infirmarer and his staff failed to save his life.

---

[3] (Cistercians) 'may not have sculptures anywhere; we may have paintings, but only on crosses; and we may have crosses made only of wood.' *Summa Cartae Caritatis XXVI.*

A Cistercian monk 'leaves his body at the gates of the monastery'. When a monk died, therefore, while his soul was granted proper care and the celebration of a requiem mass, his corpse was dealt with without ceremony. Dressed in his habit, and without shroud or coffin, the monk's body was buried in an unmarked grave. Then, in some monasteries, a new grave would be dug ready to receive the next redundant frame.

The knowledge of the existence of the ivory cross had been restricted to the Abbot, and the sacrist Alban, and after William's death they reached the conclusion that, still in its valise, it should be buried with him. It was the sacrist's sense of duty and of values, however, which ensured that a marvellous work of art was not lost to humanity forever. He made an entry in his Gesta Sacristarum[4] to the effect that a crusader had been buried with 'King Richard's cross'.

---

[4] The record of 'deeds done' by sacrists. It is of interest that in the 12th century there existed a ritual which included the burial of a cross, together with the Host.

CHAPTER 11

'Sorting Out'

The country which was to be host to the body of an ex-chaplain and companion of King Richard and a masterpiece in walrus ivory for centuries to come, had been and was to be a land of diverse peoples and riven with conflict.

Originally settled by itinerant herdsmen from the Kazan and Kirov areas of Russia, Hungary then contained both Slav and Germanic tribes as well as immigrants from north of the Black Sea. Its early history abounds with internal wars and large-scale raiding from outside its borders. By the end of the 10th century the ruling family was Christian, and King Stephen, who was crowned on Christmas Day 1000 and who ruled until 1038, succeeded in establishing a long period of peace and stability. He was canonised in 1083.

After Stephen, though, Hungary suffered many years of disputed rule, with assassinations and rebellion rife, and it was not until the rule of King Béla III (1173–96) that there was again a reasonable period of stability. Until then Hungary's candidates for the monarchy had sought to gain control by canvassing help from powerful foreigners, which often meant buying support with territory. By AD 1200 though, a reasonable balance had been achieved both within Hungary and with its neighbours. Immigration too had not only raised the country's population to a more significant size but had also reinforced it in quality, with a better informed landed class and a higher standard of agriculture.

Sadly, all these gains were dissipated by the Mongol invasion of 1241 by which so much of eastern Europe and Asia was enveloped in the 13th century. The country was overrun by savage hordes and half the population was killed or fled the country. This period of desolation was followed by a time of reconstruction under King Béla IV who returned from exile in Dalmatia and, together with András III, his successor, restored some degree of stability. However, by the early 1300s, András had died and there was no one of this line of Magyar rulers to succeed him so, once again, incumbents of neighbouring thrones competed for that of Hungary. This had its dangers as well as its benefits when a particular King occupied more than one throne, since in those circumstances Hungary might often be regarded as, so to speak, a less important country 'branch'. However, the first King of Hungary from the great Angevin dynasty, Charles Robert, was solely and wholeheartedly ruler of Hungary: the country's traditional enemies were quiescent and Charles and, in due time, his successor Louis presided over a golden age for Hungary from 1305 to 1382. The main contributors to the country's prosperity were the gold mines and agriculture, both traditional resources, and at the end of this period the population had risen to three million.

Although the 15th century was to see the return of absentee kings and kings with plural domains, in 1458 it also saw the beginning of something of another golden age for Hungary under the only national king to reign over Hungary since Béla IV, Matyas Corvinus, who possessed learning, art and military prowess in a truly Renaissance manner and brought greatness to Hungary. Unfortunately his territorial ambitions eventually outgrew his resources and, with his death in 1490, increasing threats from neighbours, particularly the Ottoman Turks, and internal squabbles which became serious revolts took their toll. In the 16th century Hungary became partitioned. The eastern half of the country together with Transylvania became ruled by a Transylvanian autocrat under the sponsorship of Turkey, while one of the 'plural' kings, Ferdinand of Habsburg (who became Holy Roman Emperor) ruled the western sector, known as Royal Hungary and including Croatia.

This divided nation of the 16th century was Hungary at one of its lowest points. Fighting and raiding for slaves was rife, the proper use of land for agriculture virtually disappeared and generally the countryside became waste land.

'Royal Hungary' under Ferdinand Habsburg received little of his attention. The Austro-German influence was maintained by the use of German troops to garrison forts and main frontiers and this did not endear the ruler to a very independent-minded population. The situation worsened in the early 17th century with the Transylvanian ruler, again strongly backed by Turkey, supporting a Protestant uprising against the Roman Catholic dominance of the 'upper classes' in Hungary emanating from the Habsburg rulers of the west. Plot and counter-plot continued for the rest of the 17th century.

In the end a very strong Ottoman army drove across Hungary to Austrian Vienna, but it did not stay and by the end of the century Habsburg rule again dominated. In the meantime the rival armies had devastated the country. Although Habsburg rule from Vienna continued until the mid 19th century, there was never a settled Hungary, holding as it did a mixture of Latin and German-speaking westerners being opposed on so many counts by Magyars, Serbians, Croats, Slovaks and Romanians.

There seemed a possibility that the breakdown of central government in Vienna in 1848, which had followed from the infection spread by the Revolution in Paris, might lead to a return of rule to Budapest and independence to Hungary, but this did not happen. Consequently, when the First World War broke out in 1914, Hungary found itself drawn in with Austria on the German side.

Those in Hungary who were against continued subjection to Austria were naturally equally opposed to being involved in the Great War on Germany's side. Equally the strong leftist movement in Russia, just over Hungary's northern border, was bound to strengthen the hand of the already strong left-wing agitation in the country against the war and the privations which, in Hungary, were bound to accompany it. With the end of the war, and the

removal of Austrian domination, there was still no true independence for Hungary because a large part of the country was held
by Romanian, Serb and Czech soldiers, and Russian support in
1918 meant Communist control of Hungary under Béla Kun and
his bolshevist methods. However, a strong counter-revolutionary
party emerged under Admiral Horthy and Béla Kun was driven
from office, with Horthy being installed as a caretaker regent
under the auspices of the Western Allies. His rule, however,
extended only to about one quarter of the territory that was once
Hungary and only about one third of the population: the balance
was distributed by the Allies to Romania, Czechoslovakia, Austria
and the new Yugoslavia, with fragments being allocated to Italy
and Poland.

The rump of 'Greater Hungary' which remained was confused
and torn by internal politics. The period of flirtation with Russia,
together with the largely Romanian occupation had exhausted
resources and the poorest in the population were frustrated by
the failure of their proletariat to realise its revolutionary aspirations.
At the same time, their activities had caused an intensification of
right-wing reaction made all the stronger because almost all were
in dire financial straits.

The right-wing counter-revolutionary movement led to a period
of 'white' terrorism which involved attacks on individuals and a
generally unhappy state in the country. Some degree of mollification
of the malcontents on both sides, however, was achieved in 1920
by the redistribution of land from large estates to smallholders
and this enabled a more conservative government to be installed.

This managed to achieve a degree of unification in the country by pressing for the revision of the Treaty of Trianon which had embodied the Western Allies' peace terms for Hungary and had so emasculated the nation.

Count István Bethlen, the Conservative head of government, played a careful diplomatic hand, recognising Hungary's dire need for friends outside the Balkans (it had few within) and he was successful in achieving for Hungary membership of the League of Nations. By so doing he managed to obtain a loan from the League which did much to attract other money to Hungary and there followed a few years of relative prosperity. Then came the 'Depression' led by a drastic fall in wheat prices in 1929 and the worldwide slump stretching into 1931. Bethlen resigned and his successor made no impression, with the result that Admiral Horthy (who appeared indestructible) appointed a right-wing radical, Gyula Gömbos.

Gömbos had been violently anti-Jewish but disavowed this in office (though it made his subsequent link with Fascist Italy understandable and the drift to Nazi Germany after Gömbos' death less of a *volte-face*). As always, the thin ice on which the large number of Jews in Hungary (some 750,000) knew that they trod failed conspicuously to change their commercial instincts or to deter the many Gentiles for whom they could provide a service. It seems likely that it was because of this that Hugo's ivory cross once more came to light.

In 1931 the Cistercian order (restored to legality with other monastic orders), together with other Christian organisations such as the Knights Templar and Hospitallers, were verging on bankruptcy and yet still had to try to fulfil their charitable as well as ecclesiastical obligations. Matters had reached the stage for the Cistercians in Hungary where the monasteries had to depart from the purist regulations which had hitherto distinguished them from their Benedictine brothers. As had been the case with the latter in England in the 12th century, they were forced to deal with Jewish money-lenders or to raise money by selling their very few possessions (over and above the wool from their flock, which was their normal currency). To the sacrist at Zirc came the time when, for the monastery to meet its obligations in this period of financial crisis, he had to consider approaching a money-lender. However, he was aware from the monastery records that within the monastery precincts was 'King Richard's cross'; not a monastery possession but only where it lay because of a monastery decision not to break Cistercian rules. To part with a valuable artefact (and its royal provenance would guarantee its worth) rather than to deal with usurers would have seemed surely preferable and within the original Benedictine rule which governed them.

The Abbot and the Prior would have had to agree to this proposition and, bearing in mind that the cross was in the crusader's tomb, there would have been much heart-searching. However, the cross had not been included as an earthly possession to accompany the body, as would have been the case in a pagan burial, but was solely there for concealment, from which the Christian world might now benefit.

Thus it was that the cross was disinterred and the word was spread that a valuable artefact would be available for purchase. The subsequent dealings would have had the complexion of highly secret negotiations, with much coming and going through third parties since, as things were in Hungary in the 1930s, there were few who would be prepared to reveal that they were rich enough to bid for any valuable artefact. The monastery never did discover who the purchaser was, but Zirc never fell into the hands of money-lenders.

In spite of the links with Germany over many centuries (or possibly because of some of these) when Hitler launched the German attack on Poland in September 1939, Hungary refused permission for German troops to cross Hungarian territory. In fact, at that early stage in the war none of the participating nations wanted to complicate affairs by involving the Balkan states. However, it was never going to be possible for the Balkans, with access to both Germany and Russia, to keep out of the Second World War for long, and in the end Hungary threw in its lot with the Axis when Germany attacked Russia in 1941. It was hoped at that stage that a token force against Russia would meet Hungary's obligations, but the resistance made by the USSR demanded otherwise and, under strong German pressure, Hungary mobilized in 1942 and sent all the troops it could afford to fight in Russia.

In general, Hungarians regarded the extreme right as a lesser evil than Communism, but Admiral Horthy, who was still in control of affairs, had begun to believe that the combination of the Allies and Russia was more likely to achieve eventual victory than the Nazis so that, for two years until 1944, Hungary managed to keep both the Allies and Hitler in play.

By 1944, however, Hungary had taken such great losses in Russia that it was clearly about to be in the position where it would be unable to maintain its national integrity, so Hitler offered Horthy protection, but in the form of virtual German control or complete German occupation. Horthy opted for the former but this meant that, albeit with Hungarian participation, the Nazis were able to suppress organisations, arrest whom they wished and oppress Jews as they did in Germany: and, of course, they did so. By the end of the war they had killed 550,000 Jews from Hungary, more than two thirds of the Jewish population there, and when the Germans left Hungary they took with them as much as they could in the way of loot.[1]

The Russian army chased the Germans, together with some 200,000 refugees, over the Austrian border in April 1945 and subsequently occupied Hungary, which became a soviet satellite country for the next decade. The Russians used it as a workshop for Russia, filling it with factories to produce heavy goods, when in fact its natural resources were agriculture and mining. Consequently the country could make little progress in recovering

---

[1] A vast quantity of loot from Hungary was carried into Austria by both Germans and their Hungarian associates in 1944/45 and amongst the hundreds of tons of diamonds, other jewellery, gold, silver and currency subsequently found at various locations were, for example, St Stephen's crown, his coronation robe, sceptre, orb and coronation cross together with Hungary's holiest relic, his mummified right hand.

from the devastation of war or resuming the agricultural and mining industries which had been its backbone and source of prosperity. During this period the property of churches was also expropriated by Russia and monastic orders were dissolved.

In 1956, with some relaxations in Russia under Krushchev and with a strong stand against Russia by Poland, something of a revolution was staged in Hungary. Soviet troops were withdrawn and Imre Nagy, who had come and gone as Hungarian Prime Minister for the past ten years, announced Hungary's withdrawal from the Warsaw Pact which linked it with Russia, and asked the United Nations to recognise Hungary as a neutral state. This was too much for the USSR and their tanks returned to the streets of Budapest. Soviet punishment was heavy. Nagy was abducted and executed. Many others were transported to Russia and some 200,000 refugees escaped to the West, ensuring thereby that a high proportion of its educated population was lost to Hungary. Under a puppet Prime Minister, Janos Kadar, Hungary remained a Russian satellite for another twelve years before there was a gradual move away from hard Communism.

A world war creates a vast company of shadowy figures who recognise few boundaries whether geographical, social or moral, and who gather spoils rather as jackals descend on a great kill. All nations have them but they acknowledge allegiance to none and often possess the passports of many. Some maintain themselves by selling their services as informers of various categories, some by smuggling, some by murder, some by dealing in the 'black market', some by looting under various guises, and some by a vicious cocktail of several of these ingredients. If there was any way of determining the route of the walrus ivory cross from its legitimate source in the hands of the crusader to the hands of one or more of these shadowy figures, it seems likely that this would have been discovered some fifty years ago when the provenance of the cross was a determining factor in its price and destination. In an environment of a country devastated by wars and by occupation by rival forces, where population has been decimated by both forced and voluntary migration, what happened to Hugo's masterpiece between its appearance at Zirc and when it was offered for sale by Ante Topic Mimara can only be a matter of conjecture. It remains a great good fortune for the world that it survived at all.

The possibilities are manifold. It may have been sold to a legitimate purchaser from whom (particularly if he were a Jewish dealer) it was looted by a German, or someone in the employ of Germany; it may have been looted directly from the monastery during the German or the Russian occupation; or it may have been taken either from the monastery or an earlier looter by a so-called Art Restoration Commission or similar body. The fact that Austria became the repository of almost all the treasures of Hungary after the war perhaps adds significance to the fact that the vendor of the cross, although a Yugoslav, held an Austrian passport and during the war worked at various times for the successive pillagers of Hungary, Germany and Russia.

The only near certainty is that the cross was obtained illegally in the 1950s, by Ante Topic Mimara, in the area described.

CHAPTER 12

'A Shame to Play Them Such a Trick'

The story of the Yugoslav Ante Topic Mimara, and how he might have used his membership of his country's Commission to recover looted works of art after the Second World War has been told elsewhere.[1]

There is some evidence that the Hugo cross was in the Cistercian monastery at Zirc in the 1930s and was, as portrayed in earlier chapters, still in Hungary throughout the war and the German occupation. The knowledge we have of Ante Topic Mimara makes it virtually certain that he did not obtain the cross by conventional, even legal, ways, but probably by making use of the supposed role of recovering works of art looted during the war to do some personal looting himself. The fact that neither he nor his wife was prepared, even posthumously, to disclose the provenance of such a unique work of art is sufficient comment on their sense of values.

---

[1] *King of the Confessors* by Thomas Hoving.

So the light of truth in relation to Mimara's part consists of the bare facts that he began touting round the art markets of the world in 1955 this great mediaeval treasure (together with much that was fake); that although it was generally acknowledged from the early days that its origin was almost certainly English, the British government was not prepared to assist the British Museum to purchase the cross without a guaranteed provenance, in spite of a discounted price; and that the Metropolitan Museum of Art secured the cross for $600,000 in 1963 in the fashion so dramatically described in Thomas Hoving's book.

In certain quarters much has been made of those parts of the cross which are, or could be interpreted as, attacks upon the Jewish race. Starting from this premise, it has been said that the cross was designed to exacerbate anti-Jewish feelings and to encourage physical violence against Jews.

The specific parts of the cross concerned were the large inscriptions on the vertical shaft of the cross. They are two couplets, one on the front and one on the sides. They are in Latin capitals and relate to the crucifixion and resurrection of Christ. That along the sides, translated, reads:

Cham laughs when he sees the naked genitals of his parent.
The Jews laughed at the pain of God dying.

The inscription on the front, translated, reads:

The earth trembles, Death defeated groans with the buried
    one rising.
Life has been called, Synagogue has collapsed with great
    foolish effort.

Both couplets are usually referred to by their two opening words in Latin, 'Cham ridet' and 'Terra tremit'.

In assessing the nature and purpose of these, as in other parts of the cross, it is important to relate them to their period in history. The Jews in Europe in the 12th century were scattered there on sufferance and in some instances under special protection. In this situation the attacks on the source of Christianity, albeit by Muslims not Jews, were bound to have repercussions on the attitude of Christians to non-Christians. It needs to be remembered that mediaeval attitudes were more fundamental than those of today. For example, in Bury St Edmunds in the 12th century the Jewish money-lenders lived together in one street and its name was 'Heathenman's Street'.

Europeans who 'took the Cross' to fight in the crusades in Palestine were embarking on holy wars and were incited to do so by the current Popes. This idea that crusaders were acting on behalf of God was reinforced after the success of the First Crusade, which occurred despite losing all their horses, and being very handicapped in so far as supplies was concerned – such an unlikely victory could not fail to be attributed to God 'working His purpose out'. Accompanying such 'holy wars', therefore, were polemics against all the 'unholy', and Jews came into this category. Indeed there were some who would, and did, argue that Jews, who were anti-Christ in that they had called for his crucifixion, were more of an enemy to Christians than those who were simply pagans who had never known Christ. Whenever individuals with theological influence made pronouncements to recruit for the crusades, attitudes against the Jews hardened. In 1096, at the time of the First Crusade, there was widespread violence against Jews in Vexin, Maine and in Germany; coincident with the polemics for the Second Crusade led by Louis VII of France and Peter the Venerable from the Benedictine monastery at Cluny, came further attacks on Jews in 1146/47 when they had been stigmatised as both 'equating to Saracens' and 'sub-human'. The capture of Jerusalem by Saladin in 1187, which led to the Third Crusade, implanted more bitterness into anti-Jewish feeling and there were extensive attacks on Jews in London at the time of King Richard's coronation in 1189 and in York in 1190.

Apart from the impacts of the crusades, the attitude of European Christians to the scattered population of Jews in their midst varied according to local conditions. Jews, the recognised money-lenders, were an important part of the commercial side of life in many areas. In this capacity they were tolerated, sometimes even protected by orders of the reigning monarchs, but they were always vulnerable to attack arising from some event, and almost always incited from an ecclesiastical source. It was in this way that what became known as the 'ritual murders' or 'blood libel' accusations started.

The story of William of Norwich, and the way in which Thomas of Monmouth inflated what may well have been the act of a pederast into a charge of ritual murder by Jews, has already been recounted. These allegations – that Christian children were sacrificed, sometimes crucified in a replica of Christ's crucifixion, and that their blood was ceremonially drunk – spread throughout Europe and were all too easily credited. However, it was not until almost a hundred years later that this type of accusation resulted in the killing of numbers of Jews in Germany and France.

In the 20th century there were accusations that the killing of fifty-seven Jews in Bury St Edmunds in 1190 was the outcome of a rabble-rousing sermon by Abbot Samson, and that the design and inscriptions on the Bury Cross were intended as a continuing threat to Jews to 'convert or be killed'. As to whether such a sermon was given by Samson, this is pure conjecture. It is significant that Brother Jocelin of Brakelond, who produced, during his time as a monk at St Edmundsbury Abbey, a very detailed biography of Samson between 1173 and the Abbot's death in 1211, and who recorded many minor incidents as well as giving a detailed analysis of Samson's character, 'warts and all', noted only the following incidents in 1190:

- The repurchase of the manor of Mildenhall from the King for 1,000 marks
- The application to the King for permission to expel all the Jews from the town, on the grounds that everything

in the town and within the *banleuca*[2] belonged to St Edmunds, so that either they should be 'St Edmund's men' or be banished

Brother Jocelin was a great admirer of Abbot Samson but was not blind to his faults, indeed he devoted a part of his account to 'Samson's Faults'. It seems unlikely that a fiery sermon resulting in the death of fifty-seven Jews in Bury St Edmunds would somehow pass him by.

Similarly, in the whole of Jocelin's account, there is no mention at all of Master Hugo's walrus ivory cross (which was, of course, created a quarter of a century before Jocelin entered the Abbey). It would seem that if it had been, as has recently been asserted, 'an icon of anti-Semitism' and 'used to incite the massacre of Bury St Edmunds' Jews in 1190', that 'it's as if Hitler and Michelangelo got together to make this thing',[3] it would almost certainly have found its way into such a detailed account; particularly in Jocelin's time at the Abbey, or even in his references to past events.

The only contemporary mention of a cross carved by Master Hugo is in the account of the possessions of the Abbey (Gesta Sacristarium) which relates that there was a crucifix and statues of the Virgin Mary and St John 'incomparably carved by Master Hugo' in the choir during Ording's time as Abbot. Thus the only

---

[2] Virtually 'Abbey lands'.
[3] Thomas Hoving as quoted in *The Guardian* of 29th August 2001.

evidence concerning the intentions underlying the design and purpose of the cross, lies in the cross itself, viewed against the period and environment at its inception and completion.

The main inscriptions already referred to ('Terra tremit' and 'Cham ridet') make great sense as a supporting accompaniment to the tree of life leading from Adam and Eve through the crucifixion to the resurrection. The singling out of the Jews' part in the crucifixion was not unique to the cross or the Abbey. There are many New Testament references which make the sense of them apt, and the need for brevity and the use of couplet form account for the somewhat shorthand language and use of metaphors.

A couplet, using the same 'Terra tremit' beginning, existed in the first half of the 12th century on a cross in Abbot Suger's St Denis, and it is perfectly reasonable to suppose that both Anselm and Hugo were conversant with this. It was also a normal convention with scenes of the trial, crucifixion and resurrection to have Ecclesia (The Church) and Synagoga (The Jews) in opposition so that, with 'Death defeated', the Synagogue 'collapsing' is no novelty. One other ivory cross of 1075 and a Gospel Book from Germany of fifty years earlier illustrated the equating of Ecclesia with Life and Synagoga with Death in the same way as in Hugo's cross, although the latter relies more on the 'Terra tremit' inscription for the strength of the statement 'Synagogue has collapsed'. Neither of these earlier examples was created for, nor were they instruments in, any pogrom against Jews.

As regards the 'Cham ridet' couplet, which has been construed by at least one imaginative writer as 'a gross and calculated insult' to the Jews and as being 'uniquely poisonous', it seems that here we have an attempt to provide, in couplet form, a biblical metaphor to illustrate the mocking of Christ (the cries of 'this fellow perverting the nation'; the spitting on him and the final humiliation). It would be an interesting exercise to search for an alternative biblical example, compressible into couplet form, as appropriate as that equating Ham's mocking of his father, Noah's, nakedness with Christ's humiliation on the cross.

All these things need to be regarded from the point of view of the period to which they belonged. These times were more than eight hundred years before 'political correctness' was invented. The crusades themselves were launched by, and with the blessing of, the head of the Roman Catholic Church and in the name of Christianity: thousands on both sides were cruelly done to death, in many instances whether as combatants or not. There were massacres in Palestine of Jews as well as Saracens, sometimes on the basis that Saracens were pagans, ignorant of Christ, while Jews were anti-Christ.

The other main feature of the Hugo cross which seems to provide difficulty for some is the 'titulus'; the title on the 'true' cross, which was disputed between Pilate, the Judge, and Caiaphas, the Priest. The subject of the titulus was supposed to describe the reason for the execution and Pilate wrote 'Jesus of Nazareth, the King of the Jews'.

Above the representation on Hugo's cross of the hand of God, which appears under the scene of the resurrection, there is an inscription which reproduces the biblical record of the dispute about the title and ends with the pointed last words of Pilate, 'What I have written, I have written' – so much more terse in Latin '*Quod Scripsi, Scripsi*'.

The use of the title 'King of the Confessors' on Hugo's cross in place of 'King of the Jews' has been advanced by some as further evidence of the anti-Semitic character of the cross, on the grounds that it indicated that Christians could not bear to associate Christ with the Jews. As in the original 'True Cross', the title is written in Greek, Latin and Hebrew; except that the Hebrew is not true Hebrew but appears to be written by someone with only a very rudimentary knowledge of the language. To the extent that the 'Hebrew' can be deciphered, it reverts to 'King of the Jews'. There are other mediaeval examples of this use of 'Confessors' in place of 'Jews', one with the explanatory note 'King of the Jews, that is King of the Confessors'. There are earlier texts in Latin which provide grounds for this equating of the titles, one explaining that a Judaean is one who confesses or praises, and the other that Jesus, King of the Jews 'is the emperor of those who believe in and confess God'.

Bearing in mind the convention in pictorial accounts of the trial, crucifixion and resurrection of Christ that the Church and Synagogue are portrayed as representing Life and Death, it would seem an unnecessary gentle hint to add this somewhat convoluted inscription.

This concluding part of the story of Hugo's cross has been devoted to the refutation in detail of the accusation that it was conceived and created specifically as an instrument of anti-Semitism. In reality the decisive argument must surely be the obvious absurdity of the proposition that the nephew of St Anselm and the uniquely talented Hugo (creator of the great Bury Bible, the grand bronze doors for the Abbey, and an absolutely unique Romanesque work of art) colluded to provide a specifically racist instrument for use by a macho Abbot over forty years later. Our knowledge of the persons concerned and their works, is more than enough to make the theory ridiculous. The story in the early chapters of this book cannot be far from the reality.

Glossary

Angevin	Descendants of Counts of Anjou or, more generally, inhabitants of Anjou.
Confessor	An ordained monk.
Constable	The Commander-in-Chief of forces or the Commander or Governor of a fortress or castle.
Franks	The title given by inhabitants of 'Outremer' to western Europeans.
Justiciar	The chief administrator of justice and government on behalf of the monarch.
Knights Hospitaller	Members of a military and religious order taking their name from a hospital in Jerusalem.
Knights Templar	Members of a military and religious order founded by crusaders in Jerusalem near the site of Solomon's temple.
Morse	Walrus.

Obedientary	An abbey or monastery official.
Outremer	Literally 'oversea' but used in the crusades to describe Syria and the Kingdom of Jerusalem.
Saracens	Loosely used in the crusades to describe Muslims; may be either Arab inhabitants of Syria or Turks or Kurds.

THE MAJOR OFFICIAL POSTS AT ST EDMUNDS ABBEY
12th/13th CENTURY

Strength in Monks 70 to 80

Abbot	Sacrist	Refectorer
Prior	Subsacrist	Subfectorer
Subprior	Cellarer	Pittancer
Third prior	Chamberlain	Master of the Vestry
Novice Master	Subchamberlain	Master of the Book-Press
Precentor	Almoner	Master of the Guests
Succentor	Kitchener	Wardens of the Shrine

Bibliography

(Note: Initial definite article omitted)

Abbey Church of St Edmund at Bury, M.R. James. Deighton Bell. 1895.

Atlas of Medieval Europe, Donald Matthew. Equinox. 1983.

Austria-Hungary, Geoffrey Drage. John Murray. 1909.

Benedictines in Britain, Ed. British Library. 1980.

Cambridge Medieval History, Ed. L.W. Previté-Orton & Z.N. Brooke. CUP. 1936

Christians and Jews in the 12th Century Renaissance, Anna S. Abulafia. Routledge. 1995.

Chronicle of the Third Crusade: A translation of the Itinerarium Peregrinoram et Gesta Regis Ricardi, Helen J. Nicholson. Ashgate. 1997.

Chronicles and Memorials of the Reign of Richard I: Volumes I & II, Ed. William Stubbs. Longman. 1864.

'Church and the Hungarian Court under Coloman the Learned'. *East European Quarterly XVIII*, 1984.

Cistercians: Ideals and Reality, Louis J. Lekai. Kent State University Press. 1977.

127

Cistercians: Monks and Monasteries of Europe, Stephen Tobin. The Herbert Press. 1995.

Cloisters Cross: Its Art and Meaning, Elizabeth C. Parker & Charles T. Little. Harvey Miller. 1994.

Concise History of Hungary, Miklos Molnar. CUP. 2001.

Conquest of Jerusalem and the Third Crusade, Peter W. Edbury. Ashgate. 1998.

Crusading Warfare: 1097–1193, Raymond C. Smail & Christopher Marshall. CUP. 1995.

English Historical Review No. CCCXIV – The legends and traditions concerning the origins of the Abbey of Bury St Edmunds. Antonia Gransden. 1985.

England without Richard: 1189–1199, John T. Appleby. Bell. 1965.

Estoire de la Guerre Sainte: Histoire envers de la Troisième Croisade, Ambroise & Gaston. Paris. 1897.

Gesta Henrici Secundi Benedicti Abbatis, Ed. William Stubbs. Longman. 1867.

Gold Train, Ronald Zweig. Allen Lane. 2002.

History of the Crusades: Volume III, Sir Stephen Runciman. Penguin. 1981.

History of Deeds Done Beyond the Sea: Volumes I & II, William of Tyre. Columbia University Press. 1943.

History of Hungary, Denis Sinor. Greenwood Press. 1976.

History of Hungary, Peter Sugar, P. Hanak & T. Frank. Indiana University Press/I.B. Tauris. 1990.

History of Medieval Austria, A.W.A. Leeper. OUP. 1941.

Hubert Walter, Christopher Robert Cheney. Nelson. 1967.

Itinerarium Regis Ricardi, Ed. M.T. Stead. SPCK. 1920.

Jewish Ritual Murder, John McCulloh. Speculum. 1997.

Jocelin of Brakelond: Chronicles of the Abbey of Bury St Edmunds, Ed. Greenway & Sayers. OUP. 1989.

King of the Confessors: The Quest for the Bury St Edmunds Cross, Thomas Hoving. Hamish Hamilton. 1981 & Revised Edition 2001.

Knights Templar: A New History, Helen Nicholson. Sutton Publishing. 2001.

Letters of Osbert of Clare. Ed. E.W. Williamson, OUP. 1924.

Memorials of St Edmund's Abbey. Volumes I to III, Thomas Arnold. HMSO. 1890–96.

Monastic Order in England: 940–1216, Dom David Knowles. CUP. 1966.

Monks of England: The Benedictines in England from Augustine to the Present Day, Daniel Rees. SPCK. 1997.

Oxford History of England: Domesday Book to Magna Carta. 1087–1216, A.L. Poole. Clarendon Press. 1988.

Realm of St Stephen: A History of Medieval Hungary. 895–1526, Pat Engel & Andrew Ayton. I.B. Tauris. 2000.

Reign of Cnut, King of England, Alexander Rumble. Leicester University Press. 1994.

Religious Violence between Christians and Jews, Anna S. Abulafia. Palgrave. 2001.

Richard Coeur de Lion: History and Myth, Janet Nelson. King's College, London. 1992.

Richard Coeur de Lion: Kingship, Chivalry and War in the Twelfth Century, John Gillingham. Hambledon Press. 1994.

Index